59372083614076   REFC

D0194868

WITHDRAWN

WORN, SOILED, OBSOLETE

FOUR
FEET TALL
& RISING

FOUR
FEET TALL
& RISING

A MEMOIR

Shorty Rossi

WITH SJ HODGES

CROWN
ARCHETYPE
NEW YORK

All photos are from the Luigi Francis Shorty Rossi Collection
unless otherwise credited.

Published in the United States by Crown Archetype,
an imprint of the Crown Publishing Group, a division of
Random House, Inc., New York.
www.crownpublishing.com

Crown Archetype with colophon is a trademark of
Random House, Inc.

Library of Congress Cataloging-in-Publication Data
Rossi, Shorty.
Four feet tall & rising : a memoir / by Shorty Rossi ;
with SJ Hodges.—1st ed.
        p.   cm.
1. Rossi, Shorty. 2. Television personalities—United States—
Biography. 3. Theatrical agents—United States—Biography.
4. Dwarfs—United States—Biography. I. Hodges, S. J. II. Title.
PN1992.4.R595A3 2012
791.4502'8092—dc23   2011035495

ISBN: 978-0-307-98588-0
eISBN: 978-0-307-98589-7

Printed in the United States of America

Book design by Lauren Dong
Jacket design by Laura Duffy
Jacket photography by Cigars International

10 9 8 7 6 5 4 3 2 1

First Edition

It's impossible to dedicate this book to
just one person. So many people have influenced
my life. So, instead, I dedicate this book to my
six pit bulls: Geisha, Mussolini, Bebi, Hercules,
Domenico, and Valentino.

If it wasn't for them, I would not be who
I am today.

Contents

FOUR
FEET TALL
& RISING

Prologue

I've got a big mouth.

I came out of the womb wailing and I've pretty much been yelling ever since. Over the years, I've learned some choice words, and I use them with abandon. Swearing adds some flavor to the yelling. Swearing is like putting whipped cream with a cherry on top of all those regular words. You get more for your money. Swearing is an art.

So I swear and I yell. A lot. I've got opinions and I make them known.

And yeah, I'm not an idiot. I know my big mouth isn't the first thing people notice about me. I'm short. Shorter than most but taller than some, and in a world where short ain't shit, you gotta do something to make sure you don't get swept underfoot. Hence my big mouth. It's gotten me into trouble and it's saved my ass, and while it may not be the first thing you notice about me, I guarantee it'll be the thing you most remember.

It's this mouth that leads people to believe I've got a Napoleon complex. Like I'm overcompensating for my perceived handicap. Napoleon complex, my ass. That bastard was five-six—what'd he have to complain about?

Plus, I got good reasons to yell.

I yell 'cause somewhere in a Los Angeles basement, there's a pit bull with duct tape wrapped around her muzzle, being trained to kill while money changes hands. I yell 'cause on some news program in Denver, there's a politician demonizing pit bulls to further his own career. I yell 'cause some punk in Tampa's got his fifth box of pit puppies and I know they'll end up in the last cage of an animal shelter before they're two. I yell 'cause humans can be the most brutal and heartless animals on the planet. I yell 'cause a pit bull can't and somebody needs to.

I yell 'cause pits are my family.

We are the same breed. We are short, muscular and stocky, misunderstood, and much maligned. We've got hard heads, short hair, and our "bad" reputations precede us every time. We are judged by the actions of a few. We are treated like the enemy before we even make your acquaintance. We are feared. We are banned. We are excommunicated.

Pit bulls and ex-cons, we got a lot in common.

Except, I don't wear my heart on my sleeve, and I've got no patience for stupidity. I can't sleep all day and I much prefer a good cigar and red wine to a bowl of mashed beef. I might stand at crotch level but I'm not gonna sniff you. And trust me, if you raise your hand to me, I won't be the one ducking and cowering.

On second thought, I guess, in most ways I'm not like a pit at all.

They're much, much nicer than me.

1

The Little
Baby Born

I was ripped from my mommy's womb on the 10th of February, 1969, in a doctor's office in West Covina, California. My mom is a Little Person, and Little moms just aren't big enough for a baby's head to be delivered naturally, so like the three kids born before me, I came by C-section.

First in the lineup was my sister Linda, born in 1960. She was what Little People call tall, what others might consider to be of average height, and from the nuts of a different daddy, a fact I discovered much later when I was in prison and started researching my genealogy, digging into my family's past to try to understand how I ended up behind bars and why I was the way I was. I found a birth certificate and a marriage license that proved Linda was born two years before my parents even met and married. It wasn't the only secret I unearthed. There were lots and lots of secrets.

Another of those secrets was Michael, a baby boy born less

than two years after Linda. Michael's baby picture hung on the wall of our living room, a constant reminder that Dad's first son had died young, barely two months old, of pneumonia. But the truth was Michael didn't die of pneumonia. Michael died of double-dominant syndrome. Michael inherited two "bad genes," two dominant achondroplasia (dwarfism) genes—one from Mom and one from Dad. Usually a baby that is double dominant doesn't even make it to delivery. The mom miscarries or there's a stillbirth. But Michael somehow beat the odds and made it to the world just in time to leave it again.

So Mom and Dad got back in the bedroom and tried again, and on December 18, 1963, my sister Janet was born. Like my sister Linda, Janet was born tall. The chances were fifty-fifty that the babies would come out "normal." Mom and Dad rolled the dice three times and won twice. They were so proud. Two tall daughters. Success.

Why they waited another six years, until 1969, before they had me, I don't know. They were Catholic but that didn't mean Mom wanted a big family. Babies are usually hard on Little women. Most of them have at most one or two kids 'cause they suffer from so many miscarriages and problems. But I guess Dad always wanted a boy. Having lost Michael, and with the odds in his favor, he decided to roll the dice one more time. Plus, Mom had handled her other pregnancies without much trouble, so it seemed like everything would work out again.

I was the heaviest baby of all. Eight pounds plus. They knew the minute I came out that I had achondroplasia. It's easy to tell, trust me. You know if you have a dwarf child.

Back then, there was no way to predict such a birth. Now, doctors can diagnose dwarfism in the womb, giving parents the option to terminate pregnancies. They can even spot the chromosome that indicates double dominance. Now, even dwarf parents, who would be least likely to care if their child is Little, can still choose to terminate a double-dominant pregnancy. There will be fewer and fewer of us walking this Earth. There already are.

I was a third-generation Little Person, the son of dwarf parents and the grandson of a maternal dwarf grandma. Being third generation, my diagnosis was dismal. The more a dwarf reproduces, meaning the same dwarf, the weaker the genes, the more chances to trigger a double-dominant gene. The doctors told Mom and Dad I wouldn't live long, and even if I did, they predicted I'd have severe physical limitations, suffer from limb deformities, and be in constant pain. They basically pronounced me handicapped, useless, and dead. They were wrong.

This is why other Little People are shocked when they find out I'm third generation. I should be dead or deformed, and I'm not. I was so physically fit when I was a kid—young and active—it actually caused resentment. Some first-generation dwarves are all fucked up physically. They've got back problems and leg problems. They walk with braces, crutches, canes, or are stuck in wheelchairs. I was supposed to die young. I didn't. I am a rarity.

Looking back, I wonder if my birth was the moment when Dad gave up on me. He'd grown up the only Little Person in a family full of tall people and he was ashamed of his size. He suffered from a bad case of self-loathing. He saw himself in me; his troubled legacy continuing against his will. Of course, that was never said to me. God forbid the truth be told. No, instead I was told that Dad was happy as hell when I was born. He'd always wanted a boy. He just didn't know he was gonna get this wonderful specimen.

His entire family descended from a brood of big, bad revolutionaries based in San Antonio, Texas. His great cousin, by marriage, was Jim Bowie, defender of the Alamo, and his grandmother was Anna Navarro, a woman considered to be a serious agitator in the Texas revolution. The Navarros were from Corsica originally, Italians, with some Spanish blood mixed in. The Rossis were also Italian, but northern Italian, with a last name referring to the plural form of the Italian word for "red." They named my dad Melvyn Louis Rossi. He hated his name. He went by Sonny instead.

There was no history of dwarfism in their family tree, so when Dad was born the son of two tall parents and the sibling of four tall sisters, he was considered a genetic malfunction. He had a broad, high forehead, a pointy chin, and prominent ears. In profile, his dwarf features were even more noticeable. He had a face as concave as a waxing moon. Dad had a typical dwarf nose, upturned and somewhat hooked at the same time. His hands had a kind of built-in V between the third and fourth fingers. It was not something easily seen, but his plump, short fingers didn't quite close together. They had to be forced. His legs were slightly bowed.

They'd never seen the likes of him before. Born in 1936 and growing up in Texas in the '40s and '50s, Dad faced the same kinds of problems that black folks were facing: blatant prejudice and discrimination. Much worse than anything I'd ever have to handle. And it wasn't just that he battled it in the world. He came home to it every day. Though his mom, Elsie, was a practicing Catholic and Italian who raised her kids to believe in the importance of family, she couldn't control the actions of her husband. My grandfather made my dad's life a living hell. Which is why we were told he was dead; that he died before any of us kids were born. This turned out to be another one of Dad's secrets. His dad wasn't dead. He didn't die until the 1990s, but Dad never spoke a word about the man.

My mom's childhood was a bit easier. She was born in Los Angeles but 'cause her mother was Southern, she was given a Southern name: Dixie Lee Brown. My mom's father, whose name was either Fred Stevens or Chester Brown—depending on which birth certificate he was using at the time—was over six feet tall. Her mom, my grandma, Mary Brown, or Nonnie, stood only three-foot-seven. They were a married couple working in the circus, though I'm not sure which company. By the time they had Mom, Nonnie and Fred/Chester had retired from circus life. Tragically, Fred/Chester died of tuberculosis nine years after Mom was born, around 1945. Mom only half remembered him. Nonnie never remarried.

Mom and Nonnie looked like each other, and for the most part, I looked like them, too. We all had round cheeks and chins, wavy, sandy-blond hair, the same smiles and the same pudgy, triangular noses. In a world where we were different, we could look at each other and see similarity. It was a great gift. One that Dad never experienced as a kid.

So, at seventeen, he left his family in Texas and moved to Los Angeles. L.A. was, and still is, more accepting of Little People than most of the world. It was the home city of Billy Barty, a well-known film actor who founded the organization Little People of America. There was always work in Hollywood for Little People. Back then you weren't a doctor or a lawyer, you were a Munchkin. You wanted to be a Munchkin 'cause it paid well. You couldn't get a job doing other things unless it was demeaning or hard labor, and none of them paid like Hollywood. So most Little People moved west with dreams of tap-dancing down the Yellow Brick Road.

Dad had no such intention. He'd always wanted to be a mechanic, but growing up, he had to hide his tools under his bed 'cause his dad would beat the crap out of him for wanting to work a real job. He just figured his son was a circus freak. That he shouldn't have any hopes for anything other than a life of freakdom. Grandpa must have thought he could beat the mechanic out of Dad, but it didn't work. Dad got his first job with Lockheed. He was hired as a riveter for airplanes 'cause he was able to fit into the small places. How he met Mom, I'll never know. They never talked about their relationship or their past. The only thing I knew for certain about their marriage was that Mom was treated more like a slave.

Dad preferred a regimented life; we all had to work and live around his schedule. Dinner was always at five o'clock. No matter what. God forbid Mom was one minute late with his dinner, and if I dared to show up at 5:10 p.m., I wasn't allowed to eat. There was no talking or laughter around the table. Dad would just inhale his food as if eating was a task to get done so he could go sit in front of the TV. There was no meaning or purpose or feeling behind anything he did.

Mom was not a modern-day, feminist woman. She woke up earlier than Dad, made sure his coffee was going, and packed his lunches. I can still see him coming home after work and sitting in the breakfast nook where Mom had his beer and his chips and his salsa ready and waiting. She'd take off his shoes and socks. She waited on him, hand and foot. Her reward? Verbal abuse. And though we never saw him hit her, me and my sisters, we all knew he beat on her. We could hear them fighting in their bedroom. We could see the results.

Verbally, he was just as abusive to my sisters but physically, no. They were fearful of him, even though they were twice his size. When it comes to control, size doesn't matter. Intimidation is a powerful motivator. Two paddles hung on our kitchen wall, one with holes and one without. They were a constant reminder that violence could happen at any second.

Dad never had to hit my sisters, 'cause he was beating the shit out of me. I might have been the biggest baby born, but I was the smallest kid growing up. That never stopped Dad from whipping the shit out of me. The spankings started when I was a toddler and they were never hidden away. The minute I did something he didn't like . . . a spanking. No questions even asked. Mom never tried to stop him. She wasn't physically abusive herself. She was a "wait until your dad gets home" kind of mother. She let him do the dirty work.

This is why I spent as much time as I could with Nonnie. I was closer to her than anyone else in my family. She loved for me to visit and stay with her. She always made sure I was entertained. She played with me and sent me cards and letters. She taught me to speak Italian. No one else ever paid much positive attention to me. Everyone else was always screaming about what I'd done wrong. I always knew Nonnie loved me. She was a warm and generous person when no one else was. Nonnie was the most, if not the only, positive influence in my daily life.

When I was really young, Nonnie was a wee bit chubby. She was diagnosed with high blood pressure and her doctor put her on a diet that worked. She lost the weight and got healthier. Dad thought Mom was pudgy, so when they visited Nonnie, he announced, "You need to teach my wife your eating habits." Right in front of everybody. Mom said nothing, but we all knew her feelings were hurt. Even as a tiny kid I understood that my dad was an asshole.

Around the time I turned four, Dad decided El Monte, California, where we lived, had become "too ethnic." The neighborhood wasn't the lily-white neighborhood it had once been, so Dad packed us up and moved us all to Reseda in the San Fernando Valley, another suburb of Los Angeles.

Now, Reseda saw its big population boom in the '50s, when a house there would cost you less than ten grand. Until the civil rights movement in the '60s, the home owners of

Reseda kept the area white, white, white. They actually had laws on the books that excluded nonwhites from owning land and houses until the Federal Fair Housing Act passed in 1968. By the time we got there in '73, not much had changed.

The houses in Reseda were all ranch style and every yard was surrounded by a six-foot brick wall. Dad was the type of person who wanted to be left entirely alone. He was the kind of guy that once he got to a friend's birthday party he wanted to leave immediately. He was so antisocial he raised the wall surrounding our house by another four feet, so no one could see inside the yard. He put screens on the outside of the house so we couldn't see in or out. He was convinced someone was gonna rob us. He lived a paranoid kind of existence, and we were all at his mercy. Trapped like prisoners in our own home.

In El Monte, Dad had been a drag racer. He spent his weekends at the speedway, racing those long-nosed, fast cars with the parachutes that pop out the back to keep them from crashing. Our backyard in El Monte had been filled with all kinds of car parts. When we moved to Reseda, the cars disappeared and were replaced by a machine shop in the garage. Dad's garage was hallowed ground. We weren't allowed in it. Not one step over the door frame.

In that garage, Dad built anything he wanted. He'd construct furniture, rebuild a carburetor, or tinker with an engine. He turned a two-wheel bike into a three-wheel bike and custom-built his own little motorcycle. If he'd wanted, he could have built a house from scratch, but Dad had no interest in customizing our house. Every Little Person learns to customize the things around them in order to live a more comfortable life, but Dad only improved those things that he himself used, like the dragsters. Despite his talents, he wouldn't retrofit our house. Instead of tearing up the kitchen and lowering the counters, we had to use stools or step-ladders. When I visited other Little People's houses, they could stand on the floor and easily reach their tables, their cabinets, their couches, their TVs. My dad refused to make any changes. He could have easily worked around Linda and Janet's needs and included them in whatever plans he made. But Dad never wanted to admit he was a Little Person and he wanted every-thing to look "normal"—outside and inside.

Mom enrolled me in kindergarten at Blythe Street School and I stayed there through sixth grade. I hated Blythe Street. I was teased, and the teachers were cruel. There was one teacher, Mrs. Taylor, who'd swat me on the hand with her shoe. She did that one too many times. Finally, I took off my shoe and clocked her in the head with it. My nasty disposition, it started way back when. Needless to say, they moved me to another class.

It was in third grade that my dwarfism became impossible to ignore. All the other kids had growth spurts and I sort of stayed put. Their fingers lengthened, my fingers stayed plump. Their faces lost the last traces of baby fat, my cheeks stayed pinchable. Their legs shot up to their hips while my knees bowed like a cowboy, as I posed for the 1977 Mrs. Titmus Grade 3 class photo. I may have outlived the doctor's procla-mation at my birth, the one that said I'd die before I saw my toddler years, but I hadn't been able to escape his more accurate prediction: that I might suffer from malformed bones or abnormal bone alignment. My arms and legs refused to grow. I could walk and I could run and I wasn't handicapped in any way, shape, or form, but that didn't stop the kids from choosing me last for any game we played. That didn't stop them from staring and whispering and keeping their distance. The kids, my classmates, stopped being innocent kids and started being nasty bullies.

I began acting out, always getting into trouble, putting tacks on the teacher's chair just to stir up some fun. I was never the highest performer in the class, so I masked my frustration by becoming the class clown. I had it in me to be good, but no one ever asked that side to show itself. I was a smart-ass with my family, too. At the grocery story, I'd knock shit over or I'd yell, "Mom, pull out your teeth!," 'cause Mom wore a partial upper denture. I don't know why I found it so fascinating that Mom didn't have teeth, but I just couldn't get enough of teasing her about it. Either of those acts got me a beating "when we got home."

I was ten or eleven the morning I discovered Dad also wore dentures. I had to go bad, but my sister was in our shared bathroom. I snuck into Mom and Dad's room to use their toilet instead. I figured they were asleep; they wouldn't hear me. But stepping into their room was a big no-no. We were never allowed to go in there. On the sink was a jar with a full set of teeth floating around. It freaked me out so bad, I yelled out, "Who's the one without the fucking teeth?" Mom woke up and whispered to me, "Don't wake your father." I knew I was in serious trouble, but I didn't care. I wanted an answer. I kept yelling, "Mom! Smile! Open your mouth!" until she finally did. Then I knew the truth. Dad had no teeth. When he woke up, I got a serious whipping. It was totally worth it. For the rest of our lives, every time I wanted to piss him off, I'd goad him with a "What's the matter? You put Preparation H on your dentures this morning?"

My parents decided to take me to Little People of America events so I could meet other Little People and their families. These events started back in 1957 when Billy Barty got on TV and made a national public appeal for all Little People in America to join him for a gathering in Reno, Nevada. Twenty Little People showed up and Little People of America was formed.

The basic mission of that nonprofit group was, and still is, to organize parties and gatherings where people under four foot ten can meet. They also do parent and peer support, adoption, medical education, scholarships, and grants. They also publish a national newsletter so everyone can brag about themselves or gossip about each other. In all, Little People of America has about seven thousand members with some seventy local chapters that meet on a regular basis.

Dad hated the events, as he was in complete denial about being a Little Person, but Mom must have convinced him I needed a wider community of support. She thought maybe the camaraderie would help me settle down and stop being such a menace. I made a friend named Danny Norvall. He lived in Van Nuys. We went to a Little People BBQ on Labor Day and a Little People Christmas party. My dad drew the line at the annual Little People Convention. It wasn't until I was older that I realized the convention was a booze- and fuck-fest. If I'd known that earlier, I probably would have begged to go, but by the time junior high school rolled around, I wanted no part of the Little People community. Everybody just sat around complaining about how miserable they were physically or how hard school had been for them. To make matters worse, everybody gossiped about everybody else. If a Little Person farted in L.A., another Little Person in New York heard about it.

I found no comfort among my people. Where I found comfort was among animals. My sister Janet had a dog named Pepe, a mutt who'd been around before I was even born. Pepe was diagnosed with a tumor, and Dad was too cheap to pay for the surgery, so we buried Pepe in the backyard. It wasn't a traumatic loss for me. Pepe had always been Janet's dog.

Then Mom bought a chocolate brown Doberman and named her Coco. She was a beautiful dog. She had a sleek coat and light brown "boots" on each of her four paws. I loved that she would nuzzle her warm brown nose against my neck and stare at me with her soulful eyes. The fur around her eyes was lighter and made her look as if she had brows.

Dad may have been too cheap to save Pepe's life, but somehow he found the money to crop poor Coco's ears. I was flabbergasted that he agreed to spend that money on a dog. He was so tight; he couldn't shit a greased BB. We'd go to a restaurant and he'd leave forty-three cents on the table. I knew we'd never be able to go back there, or they would spit in our food. He saved every penny he made, out of fear. He was terrified that medically something would happen, and he'd be broke. So I was shocked when he even willingly paid for Mom to take Coco to obedience training.

When Dad was around, Coco was never allowed inside the house, though I'd sneak her in occasionally so we could sit on the brown plaid couch and watch TV together. I got close to Coco. I played with her in the backyard. When things got heated in the house, I'd crawl into the wooden doghouse beside her and fall asleep. It was pretty comfortable with all the blankets I put in there for her bedding. Coco liked to hide under a white sheet and pretend I couldn't see her. Eventually, Mom would walk outside, find me and Coco tangled up side by side, and make me sleep in my own bed. If I could have lived in Coco's doghouse, I probably would have.

On every family vacation, it was me and Coco in the back of the AMC Hornet wagon—and by "family vacation," I mean Dad's idea of a vacation: camping, fishing, and hiking. I hated camping. I hated fishing. I hated hiking. Dad would yell at me on the boat 'cause I wouldn't shut up. I was bored out of my mind. One time he hit me so hard, I thought for sure he was gonna knock me overboard. I got so mad I threw my pole into the damn lake.

The only other vacation we took as a family was to see his mom and sisters in Texas. His sister Margie was very wealthy. Her husband owned an air-conditioning business and they had a huge house. I loved visiting my grandma Elsie in Texas. She was a tall woman with a big smile, pointy nose, and bright eyes. She loved to give me hugs. I knew when we stayed with Elsie, we were gonna get some good, traditional Italian food, and that she would let me sip her wine. We'd get to sleep in real beds and there'd be no cheap meals around a campfire. Plus, I learned a lot from Elsie. She talked to me like I was an adult and not a kid. I liked being with her.

I was also lucky enough to get to travel with Nonnie before she was confined to a wheelchair. Nonnie worked as a secretary at the World Vision headquarters in Monrovia, California, for years and years. She was on a set salary, and her rent was paid by the company. They were very good to her. They even paid for her to take vacations. When I was four, she took me to Italy, but I was too young to remember anything about it. When I was twelve, Nonnie asked if I wanted to go to Canada with her. My sisters didn't wanna go. They were teenagers and too cool to hang with their grandma. Me, I was way into British crap at that point, so I said, "Hell, yeah!" I thought if I went to British Columbia, I'd get to have four o'clock tea.

We took the train from Los Angeles to Seattle, stayed in Seattle for a few days, and went to the top of the Space Needle. Then we took a ferry from Seattle to Victoria, British Columbia. Nonnie knew I loved trains, so she took me to a museum that told the whole history of the steam engine. I loved it. I wanted to stay at the Empress Hotel 'cause there was a huge castle in the water but we stayed at the Best Western instead. We went to a restaurant called The Gatsby that had a Roaring '20s theme. I was impressed with how clean the city was, how they even hung flower pots from the street lamps. When we came back through customs into the United States, I mouthed off to an agent, and told him to get his hands off my bag. Even at twelve, my lovely personality was already in place, but I never, ever argued with Nonnie. Not once.

■　■　■

Living with Dad and his cheap-ass, racist ways, I used to daydream about how I was gonna break free, own my own house, buy this or buy that, and have the best of everything. It's not like we wanted for nothing. We had everything we needed, but it was always from a thrift store or was the generic brand or a thousand years old. The most expensive room in the house was the garage, his domain. We were treated like second-class citizens while Dad had the best.

I decided, if I ever wanted to make good, I'd have to become a lawyer or a businessman. I wanted to be part of the corporate world. I wanted to own my own company, and I wanted to be in charge. I was obsessed with a British TV show about a department store and the people that worked there. They had a corporate executive room and I could just picture my own executive room and my corporate office. I wanted my own British butler. I loved *The Jeffersons*. I was inspired by George Jefferson and how he succeeded and took over the world. I watched *Falcon Crest, Dynasty,* and *Dallas.* All the early '80s shows were about greed. I thought in order to get ahead

I had to step on somebody else. I used to tell my friends, "I'm gonna conquer the world. Imagine me as president!"

For Halloween, I never wanted to be a superhero. I wanted to be a businessman. One Halloween, I was so inspired by J.R. Ewing on *Dallas* that I dressed up as an executive cowboy. I wore a white button-down shirt, dress pants, and a matching vest with a tie. I finished off my ensemble with a straw cowboy hat, sporting peacock feathers in the band. Every time I yelled, "Trick or Treat!" I had to explain who the hell I was.

I decided to make good on all these Halloween costumes and open my own business. I knew money was my ticket out of that house, and Dad didn't give any of us an allowance, so I had to find another way to save money. I saw an opportunity at pet stores. Pet stores always needed mice, either to sell as pets or to sell as food. I went to the library and read books about how to raise and care for them. Dad was okay with me having a room full of mice 'cause it was a job. If they'd been pets, it would have been a whole other story.

I made enough money that I could buy a couple of parakeets and finches. I went back to the library and started researching how to care for them and breed them. I built an elaborate set of cages in the backyard to house them. At one point, I had twenty birds and an aviary in the yard. My mom got really into it too, and helped me care for them. The only animals she wouldn't help me with were the garter snakes. When I started keeping them, the rest of the family steered clear.

With the money I made, I opened my first bank account at California Federal Bank on Sherman Way in Reseda. I was underage, so my parents had to set it up and cosign on all my deposits and withdrawals. ATMs were new, and Mom and Dad weren't too keen on that, so to get money out of the bank I had to forge Mom's signature on the slips. It took me a while to figure out that if I had an ATM card, it would be much easier to get my money. I forged Mom's name one last time and applied for it. I had to check the mail every day to make sure my parents didn't intercept the card. It came in the mail, and I was in business. I deposited the money from the birds and mice, but I spent it as fast as I could make it. I was a Michael Jackson fanatic. I had to get his *Thriller* album. I was still into trains and had an elaborate train setup in the backyard. And, of course, I had to buy a bike. My parents got suspicious and checked my bank account. I lied and said the bank stole my money. They didn't buy it. I got the ass-whooping of my life.

I also used some of the money to buy a typewriter. In my mind, having a typewriter was an essential component of being a businessman. I even typed out corporate rules for my future company. Rule Number One was I'm The Boss. Rule Number Two was Everyone Has to Dress Up. I began insisting on wearing suits to school. Inspired by an old 1920s photograph of Nonnie's dad, my great-grandfather, I bought my first fedora. I didn't know it yet, but I had just determined exactly who I was gonna grow up to be: a businessman wearing black suits and fedoras. It just took me a long time to get there.

My dad hated my new persona. He wanted me to become a mechanic. He wanted to teach me how to build things. I wasn't interested. I didn't wanna get my hands dirty. I didn't want oil all over my suits. Dad would announce, "When you're old enough, I'm gonna get you a job at Lockheed." I didn't want a job at Lockheed. "There's good money, good benefits, good insurance." Dad had full medical coverage. We had a house, a roof over our heads, and food on the table. But we were all miserable. I wanted no part of it. To straighten me out, Dad took to berating me with "faggot," convinced I wasn't manly enough 'cause I didn't wanna work with my hands. He threatened to throw out my typewriter, so I stored it under my bed, just like he'd had to do as a kid with his tools. And just like his dad, he beat the shit out of me anytime I did something he deemed "gay." My dreams of opening a business had to stay hidden.

To get Dad off my back, I took a job at the Exxon gas station down the street from my house. I pumped gas for tips, and I met this young guy who worked there, Richard. I was in the Cub Scouts, believe it or not, and he'd been an Eagle Scout. He was into guns, and used to make his own ammunition. He taught me how to make homemade ammunition and had me label the baggies .22 or .45, and then he'd sell the shells at gun shows.

Richard was much older than me, twenty-one. I have no idea why my parents let me run around with a guy that much older. Dad was probably relieved to see me pumping gas instead of typing memos. Whatever the reason, they let me travel to gun shows with Richard or go out target shooting. The first time I shot a gun, I almost shot his girlfriend's foot off. I couldn't aim, and I didn't realize there would be a "kick."

Richard wanted to take me on a hunting trip. I never wanted to kill an animal, but any excuse to get out of the house was a good one.

We drove somewhere out in the mountains. I got a shot off and was able to kill a deer. But I didn't see any sense in it. I told Richard I didn't wanna go hunting anymore. I said, "Let's go shoot shit. I'd rather shoot a damn car window, just to destroy something, just to make noise, before I ever shoot another animal." He didn't get it. He didn't understand me. But me, I felt like . . . to hell with humans. I'd rather be with Coco than talk to a fucking human. I'd rather live my life alone with dogs than with humans. He threw that deer in the back of his old, red-ass Ford, then he dropped me off at the house. I didn't eat the deer, and I never went hunting again.

■　■　■

By the time I was in sixth grade, Reseda was a changed town. All the blue-collar union jobs were disappearing, and the neighborhood was slipping from middle class to working class. White families were moving away and Latino immigrants were moving in. Income levels went down, gangs started sprouting up, and the schools emptied. The city started busing kids from Pacoima into Blythe Street School to keep the doors open.

As everything around him changed, Dad's racism reared its ugly head again. I was allowed to have friends over to the house as long as they were white. It never made sense to me. How could a Little Person be a racist? How could Dad be a racist when he'd been judged his whole life for being a midget? He knew what it was to be treated differently.

Nonnie taught me that everyone was the same. She never had a racist bone in her body; she wasn't raised that way. Maybe having parents that worked in the circus, she met different people, and that gave her a more open mind. However she came to her opinions, it didn't matter. She passed her acceptance of diversity on to me and I listened. My dad may have been a racist ass but Nonnie's influence won out. I became friends with Sean and Oscar.

They were Mexicans from Pacoima. It was like they were from another world. They felt different like I felt different. I couldn't do everything the tall kids could do. The gap between me and my classmates had widened into a chasm. Before the Mexican kids showed up, I was basically alone with my difference, and when you get treated differently, you act differently. Once Sean and Oscar showed up, it was like my people had arrived. They understood that I understood what it was to be different in an all-white suburban school. A bond of friendship began, and the closer I got to Sean and Oscar, the more my white friends drifted away. Not that I had so many to drift.

I wasn't even close to my own sisters. They were so much older than me, they considered me a child, not a brother. If Mom and Dad left the house, they made Linda or Janet babysit me. Both sisters saw me as a nuisance. I did my best to live up to their expectations. I gave them hell. Tearing around the house, running off into the neighborhood and making them chase me through the streets, slapping and hitting them, walking over their board games and kicking all the pieces loose, changing the TV channels. I always got a beating when Dad got home.

By the time I got to sixth grade, my sister Linda was in high school and she'd become a real slacker. She ditched school and smoked weed. Janet was the exact opposite. She was Little Miss Prissy Straight-A Student. She never got in trouble. Me and Linda tried to get her to smoke a cigarette once so we would have some evidence against her. She wouldn't take a puff.

My parents were oblivious to what was going on in my sisters' lives. Linda had always been Mom's little girl and Janet was always Dad's little girl, so me, I became the mutt of the family. Dad couldn't turn me into a mechanic and I sure as hell wasn't the sports jock he'd hoped for, so he just wrote me off. I was on my own.

Until I found my gang.

2
White
Blood

They called me Mr. Automatic. That first year at Northridge Junior High was the time of my life. I loved the school dances, and I'd dance my ass off. I got lots of attention for it, which I liked, and I even got my first nickname: Mr. Automatic, 'cause I'd shaken my shit to the Pointer Sisters song "Automatic," and made a big impression. I was named Class Clown in the yearbook, and I even convinced the coach to let me play football—even though everyone was scared to death I'd be killed. I could run pretty fast and when the guys tried to tackle me, they'd jump too high and catch nothing but air. By the time they hit the ground, I was gone. My nickname changed from Mr. Automatic to Shorty, and for a few games, I did pretty well. Until the other teams figured out how to triple-team me with a tackle, and that was too much for me. I had to give it up.

From there, the train went off the track. I opted for special ed classes 'cause my friends, the jocks, said they were easy, and

I wouldn't have to work too hard for decent grades. I started getting into more and more trouble. Fighting. Detention hall was my second home. I was becoming defiant. I became a master of lies. Sean and Oscar had been shipped to a different junior high, so I'd take the bus from Reseda to Pacoima to hang with them once in a while. I had a friend, DeShawn, who went to a different junior high in South Central L.A. On the weekends, me and DeShawn would head out to Malibu to drink, smoke pot or cigars, and meet girls. I'd be the only white guy on the bus, but it didn't faze me. Everyone would stare. I figured they were looking 'cause I was a midget. It took me a long time to realize it was 'cause I was white and they were worried I'd get my ass killed.

By the end of seventh grade my whole social circle had changed, I was best friends with Cerisse and Little Al. I called them my Godsister and Godbrother, even though I had to keep my friendships with them a secret from my family. All my friends were either black or Mexican, and that was unacceptable in my house. It was just better to do my own thing and lie and say I was with my old friends, the white friends I never saw anymore.

Over the course of the next two years, things at home got much worse. Dad had such strong views about how I should be living my life, and I was hardheaded. I didn't wanna hear it. Which meant more beatings and constant verbal abuse. I wasn't a saint, not even close to it, but I didn't wanna keep living with Dad's constant bullshit. To come home every single day and be cussed at, yelled at, beat on . . . it was too much. I never, ever wanted to go home.

I confided in Cerisse and Little Al about my home life. Cerisse kept saying, "My mom says you can come over." It was a risky thing for her mom, Mama Myrtle, to offer. She could have been seen as a black woman kidnapping a white kid. I kept her offer as a backup until finally, in ninth grade, I'd had enough of Dad and said, "Fuck it, I'm gone." I ran away to the projects to stay with Mama Myrtle, Cerisse, and Little Al. School was only in session for a few more weeks before summer break. My parents reported me as a runaway. They didn't know where I was staying. Nobody had cell phones yet, so there was no way for them to get ahold of me. For a few weeks, I was free.

I stayed at Mama Myrt's through most of June before I called my sister Janet to let her know I was okay. She was married now and living in Palmdale. She tried to convince me things would get better at home. I didn't believe her. No way was I going back. Then she said, "Mom and Dad know where you are, and they're gonna send the police in after you." I didn't wanna hurt Mama Myrt and her family. They were hiding me, essentially, and it wouldn't look good. This was before the riots sparked by the Rodney King verdict, and the Los Angeles police were considered vicious and out of control. I didn't wanna cause a problem for Cerisse's family. I talked about it with Mama Myrt. She encouraged me to stay. She wasn't afraid of the police, but my mind was made up. I didn't want to cause her any grief. Mama Myrt gave me a hug and told me, "Come back whenever you want, Shorty."

Dad sent Janet to come get me. She was scared out of her pants. The projects were not the friendliest place. Janet just wanted out of there, so I packed up my stuff and she drove me home. When I walked in the door, Dad announced, "If you try to run away again, I'll beat the shit out of you." Things were clearly not gonna get any better. Janet returned to her family in Palmdale and I just stayed in my room and out of Dad's sight as much as I could. Then a telegram arrived at the door.

It was 1983. Late June. I was sitting on my bed when I heard it happen. A delivery guy rang the doorbell and Mom answered it. He gave her a telegram—seriously, an old-fashioned telegram—notifying Dad of his termination from Lockheed. You would have thought someone had died. A travesty! Mom started wailing. She was screaming and crying so loudly I couldn't even hear what Dad was saying. I could tell he wasn't surprised, but Mom was shocked; she hadn't seen it coming. I shut my bedroom door and pretended not to hear any of it.

The house went into crisis mode. Mom got her first and only job doing clerical work for Baskin-Robbins to help with bills, even though Dad probably had money stashed everywhere. Dad hated that Mom was working. He was the king of his castle, and now there was no slave around to take care of his castle or the king. No one to take off his shoes and socks. No one to have his salsa and chips waiting. Dad couldn't handle it. He went on an alcoholic binge, sneaking beers and disappearing to bars, saying, "Don't tell your mom where I'm going." The firing really affected him. Dad was in his fifties and his prospects for finding another steady union job weren't good. Money was his safety net and owning property was a source of pride. Losing it, or the thought of losing it, tore him to pieces.

Despite having such a rough childhood in Texas, Dad always had plans to retire to San Antonio. He constantly complained about the lack of space and privacy in Los Angeles, saying that "Texas was the greatest place" 'cause in Texas, the houses were bigger, the land was cheaper, and you got more of it, which fed into his need for isolation. This was always his mind frame, so when the Lockheed firing happened, he just "sped up" his retirement plan. Really, he had no other choice. He still had his family down there, and a job lined up through his sister Margie's husband's air-conditioning company. He'd be the on-call, twenty-four-hours-a-day, air-conditioning repair mechanic for a medical research facility that did scientific testing on monkeys. Dad announced, "All right, we're putting the house up for sale." He lied and said that he was leaving Lockheed of his own accord, and that the monkey lab job was a better job, even though I knew he was involved in some court case surrounding his firing and that he was doing community service at a nearby park. The details of his court case were kept from me. Dad and his secrets. But I wasn't stupid. I could see that Dad was in trouble.

Before summer was even half over, Dad sold the house in Reseda and bought a house in Brookvale, a tract-house development that served as a suburb of San Antonio. Really, Dad and Mom were headed for bumfuck. I wasn't going anywhere. I watched them pack and go and barely waved goodbye. I moved in with Nonnie and spent my weekends at Mama Myrt's. I wouldn't say I never gave Nonnie any trouble but I tried to keep it to a minimum. Nonnie had gotten older. She was having a lot of trouble walking, so we mostly just sat side by side and watched *The Golden Girls* together. She thought the show was too racy. We'd have a lunch or a dinner at Sambo's and I'd walk down the street beside her, trying to keep up with her scooter. She was classic in that scooter, like she might run over anyone that got in her way. Any day I spent with Nonnie was a good day.

But Mom kept hounding me, saying, "You know it's hard on your grandmother for you to be there. You're getting ready to go back to school in the fall. Why don't you come to Texas and try out the school here? It's a good school. The life here is so much nicer . . ." Yada, yada, bullshit, bullshit. She really wanted me to move to Texas, but even with a half a country between us, Dad and I couldn't get along. The minute we got on the phone, we started yelling at each other. The man was never gonna change. Texas seemed like a bad idea, but Mom was right, it was hard on Nonnie for me to be around. I didn't wanna be a burden on her any longer.

That fall, before my tenth-grade year, I moved to Texas with the mentality that I was gonna hate it. I was determined, from the get-go, not to stay in that state. I would get back to

Los Angeles at any cost. From the moment I set foot on Texas soil, I had a big "no" for the whole situation.

Texas was a culture shock. From the neighborhood to the weather to the good-ol'-boy type of mentality. San Antonio was a completely different world from Reseda or South Central L.A. There was a big military population and an even bigger divide between the white people and the brown people. Mom and Dad had a nice house, right down the street from the mall, but I didn't like it. High school was harder for me. I enrolled at Marshall High but having been educated in the L.A. Unified School District, I was way behind the other students.

I got a job at the hamburger chain Carl's Jr. I knew I needed to save up money if I was gonna leave Texas. I'd promised Mom I'd give this new life a real try, but I had no intention of staying. Though I loved being closer to Elsie and getting to spend time with her, it wasn't enough to make up for the living conditions at home. Elsie never nagged me about the clothes I was wearing or my friends. She accepted me as I was but she had no idea what I was dealing with in the house. I never told her about our fights. I guess I wanted to protect her from the truth. I got in more trouble in Texas than I ever had my entire life. There were curfew violations and detentions. I kept falling asleep in class 'cause I'd been out all night drinking with Robert.

Robert was my best friend. His family moved in across the street not too long after I arrived. Robert felt different 'cause he was a Puerto Rican in a lily-white neighborhood. We started talking one day, then we went to the mall and hung out. It didn't take long for us to start our drinking adventures. We would sneak out of our houses at one o'clock in the morning and push his parents' car down the driveway in neutral so they wouldn't hear the engine. We'd drive around, drinking for a few hours, then sneak back into our houses before our parents woke up. I never got caught. Well, almost never.

The only time I got busted for drinking, I was so stupid. I'd thrown my clothes in the dirty hamper without noticing there was vomit on my shirt. Mom found it the next morning. I got a beating, then a lecture about having my first drink. My first drink. Please. I'd been drinking since seventh grade.

After getting busted, Robert and I stopped sneaking out to drink and started taking secret flights back and forth from Los Angeles to stay with Mama Myrt. Robert's dad worked for United Airlines, so we could fly for free. I'd tell my parents we were going to Chicago to visit his family for the weekend. Instead, we'd head west. There was no caller ID, no way of verifying where the hell I was, unless I got in trouble. We actually gave my parents his grandma's number in Chicago. If they called looking for me, which they did one time, Robert's grandma covered for us. I don't know why she did that for Robert, but she did.

Robert and I flew to L.A. twice and all we did was hang around the projects and do nothing. It was a world away from Texas, that's all that mattered. I was happier there. Years later, George Lopez would tease me about it, saying, "People were trying to move on up and you were trying to move on down." He'd be right about that. I just wanted out.

The L.A. neighborhood was like a TV show, with some-thing dramatic or comedic always happening. I wasn't scared to be there. Not ever. Any other idiot in his right fucking mind wouldn't walk two feet into those projects, but I was naïve. I felt safe 'cause I was basically untouchable. I was down with the Baileys, one of the three biggest families in the proj-ects besides the Thorntons and the Hawkinses. The Baileys had fourteen aunts and uncles, and all their kids, nieces, and nephews lived within a few doors, or at most, blocks from each other. The Baileys were a peaceful family and for the most part everyone got along.

I loved Mama Myrt's house. It reminded me of visiting grandma Elsie. Mama Myrt's living room functioned as a com-munity center. Everyone went in and out all the time. All day long. At any given moment there would be fifteen or twenty people hanging out, eating, talking, sharing stories, and being a big, warm family. There were no schedules. Things happened and I could just go with the flow. That was the spirit I liked. I didn't wanna go home and pull the blinds down, shut the door, and keep the neighbors out. I didn't wanna sit down to dinner every night at 5 p.m. And most of all, at Mama Myrt's house, there was never really any arguing. If people argued, then five minutes later it was over with and forgotten.

Grandma Bailey, Mama Myrt's mother, was the matriarch, the woman in charge of the entire family. I could stop by her house at any time. She had a four-bedroom apartment, and there was a party every damn day 'cause so many of the kids lived with her. Grandma Bailey would always take care of you if you were sick, or help you out if something was going on. That kind of unconditional support was something I'd never experienced inside my own house. In Texas, I had material comforts, a white neighborhood, and safety in the streets, but in the projects, I had love, and that's all that mattered.

Having to fly back to Texas after spending the weekend with the Baileys was depressing. I never wanted to get on that plane. Robert would have to talk me into it. Life in Texas with Dad had gone from miserable to unbearable. It was the worst time in my life. Janet and Linda were both married and out of the house. It was just us Little People, but Dad kept the house as if tall people lived there. I wasn't allowed to put my bed on the floor. I had to use a stool to climb into it. My parents had a bed so high off the ground you had to pole vault to jump into it. Mom had to take a running start just to make the jump. Being at home was physically uncomfortable. I didn't wanna live my life, walking around my own home, inconvenienced.

The house had come with a microwave from the late '70s or early '80s (whenever they started making them), when they used to cost $500. It was a huge, monstrous piece of equipment that blew up and had to be replaced. Dad announced he could get a microwave for "real cheap," and that he'd install it the next day.

The next day, Mom and I came back to the house and were looking all over the kitchen for this new microwave. It wasn't on any of the counters. I said something like, "Don't you have to plug the new ones in?" when I noticed Mom staring straight up, her mouth hanging open. All she said was,

"Oh my God." Dad had installed a hood microwave over top of the stove burners, as high up as the exhaust vents. There was no way any of us could reach it without a stepladder. It was just so damn cheap and inconsiderate of him. I felt . . . resentful. I promised myself I'd never be that cheap. I'd never live in denial of who I was. I wanted to be the exact opposite of Dad.

My time in that Texas house didn't last long. I don't even remember what started the argument. Dad probably wanted me to do something and I probably mouthed off and said, "I'll do it when I'm ready." Whatever was said, Dad got mad. He was always mad. I was standing in the living room and we started going at it. Physically beating on each other. I was tired of taking it from him. I started fighting back.

The altercation ended up in the kitchen and I got so fucking fed up, I clocked him once, hard. I slammed him into the refrigerator and everything on the top shook and fell off. Mom got in the middle of it and yelled, "That's enough! That's enough! Both of you!" I ran out the door. I slammed the door so hard, the glass cracked.

I ran to Robert's house. His parents were out of town for two weeks but I knew I wouldn't be staying for long. I was going back to Los Angeles to live with Cerisse and Little Al. I'd take Mama Myrt up on her offer to "come back anytime." It never even crossed my mind to call Elsie or to move in with her. She probably would have allowed me to stay there. She had a big house and no one in it with her, but I just wanted to be back in Los Angeles with my friends.

I couldn't let my parents know of my plan, so whenever they would leave the house, I'd sneak over and pack my things. I sold my DJ set—two turntables and the whole setup, with microphones, the whole nine yards. I used the money to book a ticket on Muse Air. I bought a suitcase and boxed up the rest of what I wanted to take with me. It wasn't much.

On the morning of my flight, Robert helped me load up his dad's car. We got up super early, so Mom or Dad wouldn't see us packing the trunk. Mom came out to get the newspaper. We ducked behind some bushes and almost got caught. I watched her go back into the house. It made me sort of sad to leave her with that man, but she'd made her choice long before I was even born. She'd never leave him. Robert drove me to the airport and that was that. I was headed back to the projects for good. This time, there'd be no prodigal return. I'd been in Texas for less than a year.

On my sixteenth birthday, Mom walked over to Robert's house with a homemade cake and candles. Robert had to tell her I was gone. This time, they knew exactly where to look for me. Mom called Mama Myrt's crying for me to come home. I refused. Dad threatened to send the police, but this time I'd done my homework. In Texas, when you turned sixteen, you were legally allowed to run away. You could petition the court for emancipation. I told my parents, "If you send the police in here to ship me back to Texas, I will just run away again and again and again." So Dad just let me go. I never again set foot in that Texas house. Until I decided to reunite with my father. But that would be many, many years down the road.

windows as people chased other people with rifles and guns. I saw lots of people get shot. A body would lay in the street for nine or ten hours before the police would ever show up. They had to wait until they could gather six or seven patrol cars to come in as a force. It wasn't safe for a single police car to roll through.

It didn't take long to become numb to so much violence. That year was like watching a violent movie. I felt so distanced from what was going on, like an observer and not a flesh-and-blood person, right there in the moment. But losing Mikey was hard. It was a grim reminder that having close friends was a bad idea. Caring about people just caused pain.

Like loving Nonnie. Mom and Dad had put Nonnie in a nursing home and it was killing me to know she was stuck in that place. Yes, her body was deteriorating and she wasn't doing well, but I was fucking pissed that they'd left her to die, alone. I yelled at Mom, "She's your mother. You've got rooms! Put her in the house with you!" but Dad had made up his mind. Nonnie would rot away by herself. She was my favorite person. She didn't deserve to live like that. His actions strengthened my resolve to stay away forever. They also made it clear: if I was gonna invest in loving someone or something, it had better be a dog.

■ ■ ■

That's when I adopted my first pit bull. I named him Coco. Yes, the same name as Mom's Doberman. Mom's Coco was with them in Texas. I wanted my own dog in Los Angeles.

Coco, the pit bull, was chocolate brown, too, but a male, about six months old when I got him. I took a lot of crap for naming a boy dog Coco, but I didn't care. Coco was my right-hand man. Me and Coco were the shit going through the neighborhood. We were inseparable.

The first time I saw a dogfight was in the projects. I couldn't understand why they'd train their dogs to be mean, to be evil. I saw guys put gunpowder in their food. It did something to them and messed with their mind. They'd let them go at it and just rip each other apart until the weakest dog died. It happened on the sidewalks, in the streets. There were so many dogfights, I lost track. No one called the police. Dogfighting was just part of the culture. It wasn't hidden away. It wasn't taboo. It was out in the streets, where money changed hands.

Though they fought other breeds of dogs, the majority of the dogs used were pit bulls. They were matched against other pits of similar size and weight and conditioning. Most dog handlers thought it was "unfair" to fight a sick dog against a strong dog, although I thought it was unfair to fight them at all.

Two handlers or owners would bring their dogs into the ring or the pit or whatever area they were using. Some guy would act as a referee. If a dog was hard to handle, or bit his handler, they'd just kill it. The dogs were trained to be loyal and subservient to their owners, but to be dog-aggressive, to kill other animals. It was kill or be killed, so I didn't blame the dogs. They were just doing the job they'd been taught.

The owners would wait on opposite sides of the pit until

the referee said, "Release your dogs." Then the fight started. The dogs would be pulled off each other during the match, returned to their "corners," and then released again. Just like human boxing. Fights lasted anywhere from a few minutes to over two hours. I refused to stay and watch. I couldn't stand to see those dogs with broken legs, or disemboweled, or faces half ripped off, struggling to survive . . . I couldn't stand the cruelty. It made me sick.

During the fight, dogs had to cross over what was called a "scratch line" before a certain amount of time passed, or else be disqualified. If a dog didn't wanna fight, wouldn't cross that scratch line, he was considered a coward and he was killed. There was no need to keep him around. He wasn't a pet. He was a product. Dogs that survived or won a match were "rewarded" by having to fight again and again. If they were successful every time, they'd become stud dogs. They were money-making machines.

Everything in the projects was about money. Everyone was hustling to make an extra dollar. To survive. If you weren't selling drugs or fistfighting or both, you were a gambler. You were playing dominos or spades or rolling dice. Pit fighting was just another way to make money, but I wouldn't even think of fighting Coco. He was my best friend and you don't fight your best friend. I preferred cuddling with Coco in my bed at night.

■ ■ ■

I was still enrolled in high school . . . well, high schools. After leaving Marshall High in Texas, I went to Locke High for one semester before I got kicked out for being an ass. I got mad at one of my teachers and took a baseball bat to his car, bashed in one of his windows. My anger was out of control by then. I was shipped to Cleveland High and got busted there, so they shipped me to David Starr Jordan High in the most dangerous neighborhood for me: rival gang territory. Getting on that bus to David Starr Jordan, me and my boys, we had to stick together and practically run after the last bell rang. Getting from the front doors of the school to the L.A. Metro bus stop was a danger zone. Crips would pelt us with rocks or throw M-80s at us. Making it onto the bus was no guarantee of safety. One time, they got ahold of a fire hose from the gym, plugged it into a fire hydrant, ran onto the bus, and hosed everyone down. This wasn't a school bus. Regular people were on there, just trying to live their lives. Every day, I felt like a sitting duck. It was the most dangerous two miles I traveled in my life.

There was a teacher at David Starr Jordan who tried to make a difference. He taught economics and actually put faith in me. He was an older, baldheaded black guy. He sat me down and said, "You're smarter than you appear to be with your devious ways." He made me wanna learn more. He actually cared about his students. He was really involved not just in my school life, but also in my personal life, in everything I was doing. 'Cause of that econ teacher, I got on the Dean's List for my first semester ever. Before that, I'd never been asked to

use my talents. I had only ever gotten D's and maybe C's. He showed me I was capable of a lot more. Then someone took a shot at me and tried to kill me, so I had to leave David Starr Jordan High for good. I ended up, my senior year, at Fremont High. I dropped out, three credits short of graduation. Biology was never my thing.

As a dropout, I had a lot more free time on my hands. I had transferred from my Carl's Jr. job in Texas to a location in Los Angeles, but got fired for being late for my shifts. I wasn't interested in showing up on time. I was more interested in hanging with my roll dog, Jeremy Lucas. I called him Jerry. He was a couple of years younger than me, a friend from the projects. We were busy getting drunk, smoking weed, and getting laid. It was easy for me to get girls. Easier for me than for Jerry. There were a lot of girls who just wanted to see what it was like to sleep with a midget. I benefited from their curiosity. Once you go small . . . you never go tall.

I wasn't a committed boyfriend to any of them, not even my fiancée, Liz Evans. Liz was older than me by nine years. She was twenty-seven. I liked them older. I made it a policy to never date girls my own age or my own height. When I was sixteen, I'd hooked up with a woman who was thirty-two. In the projects, you had people of every different age hanging around each other. It didn't take much to meet them.

We'd go out to nightclubs. It was easier then to get into clubs and drink. It's harder now. I used to go to the liquor store; they never questioned me. They thought I was older. We would go to World on Wheels or Skateland USA or someone would set up their own block party and charge ten bucks. All the places were dangerous. We had to stop going to World on Wheels 'cause the Crips took it over. It had originally been a roller rink, but they'd renovated it and turned it into a dance club.

I didn't meet Liz at the clubs. She was related to the Evans family, but they weren't major players in the projects. I just knew her from around the way. We started talking and hanging out and I fell in love a little. Marriage, in the projects, wasn't taken as seriously as it should have been. Guys married and divorced all the time, so it seemed like the thing to do. She wasn't pressuring me. I was the one who decided that this was what I wanted. I was stubborn and I wouldn't take no for an answer. I was a big asshole and I got my way. I told Liz we were getting married. She said yes.

We went to the St. Vincent Jewelry Mart in downtown L.A. to get the ring. That's where we used to buy all our jewelry at the time. Gold nugget rings and gold rope chains around our necks. That was the style. I had more expensive jewelry on me than I put on her finger. My little ass could be cheap, a remnant of growing up with Dad. I bought her a band, not a diamond, and I got a matching gold band, too. We may have had the wedding bands, but we never made it to the ceremony.

The engagement lasted about four months. Liz didn't know I was sleeping around, so she kept planning the big day. We got real close to walking down the aisle before I decided marriage wasn't for me. It was a spur-of-the-moment decision to marry, and it was a spur-of-the-moment decision to call it off. It got a bit ugly. Liz heard about the other girls after we broke up. I started making sure to look both ways before crossing any street. Liz had threatened to run me over if she ever caught me in a crosswalk. Some people get pretty mad when you hurt their feelings.

Once I was disengaged and fired, I didn't have much to do. I'd get up, take Coco for a walk, watch TV, and play video games in my room. Then I'd walk over to Grandma Bailey's house or one of the other aunts' and uncles' places. I'd hang out with my buddies on 115th and wait for something to happen. Then something did. A man I'll call Uncle D. pulled up in his 280Z.

Uncle D. was literally an uncle. He was the brother of Mama Myrt, and made his money dealing crack. One night, Uncle D. rolled up and stuck his head out the window, asking, "Shorty, you wanna go for a ride?" What else did I have to do? Nothing. So I got in. We crossed the border into Tijuana into this scary-ass area. I hadn't spent any time in Mexico, so it seemed rough 'cause it was foreign to me. Uncle D. went into a raggedy-looking building, came back out, and put something in the back of the trunk. Then we drove back, through Los Angeles and all the way north to Atascadero. Uncle D. lived there with his wife. He had a whole setup in Atascadero where they made crack, divided it, weighed it, and packaged it for sale.

The first time I got into his car, I had no idea what I was agreeing to. I knew what Uncle D. did for his business, but I was just along for the ride. It didn't cross my mind that we might get busted. I didn't think about the bigger picture. I didn't think about what I was doing, or how I was getting involved. By then it was too late, I was in. People who live in the projects know what I mean. When you are surrounded by this shit all the time, it becomes part of your life. Seeing people get stabbed, killed, get the shit beat out of them, watching a carjack—you become a product of the environment. Everything you are and you do is part of what is going on around you. Only a small percentage of the people who live there make a success out of their lives. Everyone else is fucked.

From the outside, it's easy to blame people, to believe they had chances. But you're telling some kid to go work at the pool in the park and make $50 a day when he can make $500 a day selling dope. What's his option? We're a country of greed. That's what we are taught, to want more and more and more. It's not an excuse, but you have to be some super-strong kid to be in that environment and not end up like everyone else. You just don't see any other way around you. I didn't move to the projects so I could hold money for a drug dealer, and carry a pistol. I wanted to get away from my father and my family and be happy around the friends and people I liked. The more I hung around the gangbangers and the drug dealers, and the more I saw, the less illegal it seemed to me. I didn't even realize I was into dirt until I was in up to my neck.

Uncle D. brought me in 'cause he caught his own cousin stealing from him. He said, "Shorty, can you count this money again?" I counted it and told him what I came up with. He said, "No, that's impossible. That means there's $6,000 missing." I said, "I counted it three times. I know how much is missing." He said, "You counted that three times? That fast?" He sat down and counted it with me, which took twice as long as when I counted it myself three times. He goes, "You nailed it right on. How'd you do that so quick?" I had no answer for him. I was just good with numbers. That's when he offered me the job. There was no application process. This was no Carl's Jr.

He trusted me not to steal. Apparently, he'd seen me return money to some guy that dropped it on the street. That made a big impression on him. Later, he told me he'd even tested me a few times, leaving me alone with big sums of cash to see if I took a skim off the top. I never did, so for the next year, before he was arrested, he paid me $1,000 a week to count his money and track his books.

I never told anyone, not even Mama Myrt, Cerisse, or Little Al, that I was holding money or drugs for him in my bedroom. On some days, I'd have as much as $100,000 under my bed. Once a week or so, I'd travel with Uncle D. to Atascadero to sit and count out the money. I'd never seen so much cash in my life: $350,000 in cash and it wasn't in $100 bills. It was dollar bills, fives, and twenties. I begged him to stop selling nickel pieces and start selling bigger bags. All those singles got on my nerves.

You would think that I had learned my lesson all those years ago when I tricked the bank into giving me an ATM card and ended up getting beat to hell for it. But nope. I spent the money as fast as I could make it. On clothes, on jewelry, I even bought a junker of a car. That ass-whooping Dad laid down hadn't taught me one damn thing. Mama Myrt got suspicious. She asked me, "Where do you get all this money?" She kept pounding it into my head, "Don't sell drugs! Don't sell drugs!" I told her, "I promise you, I'm not." But she didn't buy it. "Then what are you doing?" I couldn't think of nothing else, so I told her, "I'm a Little stripper!" I thought Mama Myrt's face was gonna fall off, saying, "Shut up!" I convinced her that ladies would pay big money to watch a Little Person shake it and strip. It was such a crazy story, she had to believe it.

In reality, while I was working for Uncle D., I also had a job working at a law firm called Gibson, Dunn & Crutcher LLP. Even though I'd dropped out of high school, I still had my dream to be a lawyer or a corporate boss. I thought I could work my way up the ladder the hard way, no college necessary. I started out as a mailroom clerk, then was promoted into the accounting department. I had big hopes for the job. I wasn't gonna be a dealer's bookkeeper forever.

I had no interest in becoming a permanent part of the drug trade, and I considered myself on the outside of the nasty work. I knew how to cook crack, but I wouldn't do it. I knew how to sell, but I wouldn't do it. I saw a way to make a shitload of money without having to get into the real mess of dealing. So I took it. It wasn't my life goal.

The law firm was inside the Crocker Center, which is now the Wells Fargo Towers in downtown L.A. We were on the fortieth-something floor, and at night, me and my homies would go there and have meetings in the boardroom. We'd discuss where to get drunk and who to shoot. I'd started carrying a pistol in ninth grade when all my friends started carrying, and I was like, ooh-la-la, I need one, too. I had a .22 I got from my homies, but with all of Uncle D.'s money under my bed, I decided I needed something more. I graduated to a .25. I couldn't get too big a gun 'cause my fat, chubby dwarf fingers wouldn't fit through the trigger hole.

I liked feeling like a corporate boss. It was the closest I'd ever come to living out my childhood Halloween dream of being an executive cowboy. Only now, I wore red jeans and do-rags when I was off the clock. No one never said nothing about us meeting there. Of course, this was before the days of video surveillance in offices and high security. We'd leave the office and head to the bar at the top of the Bonaventure Hotel. The more we drank, the more we talked about who to shoot. We were intelligent and stupid at the same time. We looked good. We were making money, and yet, we all assumed, someday we would end up in jail. It seemed inevitable. All around us, our friends were either dying or being arrested. If it was a choice between death by drive-by or five-to-ten, jail was the better option. It wasn't something we were trying to avoid. It was the light at the end of the tunnel. The headlights of an oncoming train.

It took about a year for that train to catch up to Uncle D.

He got busted for possession, and not long after he was locked up, I was arrested myself. Not for counting his money. Or crossing the border with drugs in a trunk. Or for sneaking my homies into the law office most nights. No, the train that came barreling down the tracks at me had big-ass lights. I was arrested for attempted murder.

3

Felon

I was hanging with a bunch of idiots, four guys named Dante, Lewis, T.J., and Bernard. These were friends of mine. At least, I thought they were. We were all young, not out of our teens. I was eighteen, Bernard and T.J. were seventeen, and Lewis and Dante were nineteen. Dante and Lewis had the ugly habit of robbing people. That was their thing. Not mine. I had saved enough money working for Uncle D. that I didn't need to rob anyone, and even if I'd needed the money, I wouldn't have robbed someone for it.

The only reason I ran with Dante and Lewis was 'cause they had a truck. I had a 1978 Monte Carlo that was a piece of shit. It used a broomstick as the stick shift, and I had to crawl out the passenger-side window 'cause neither door would open, and the window on the driver's side wouldn't roll down. The car looked like it had survived a demolition derby. It wasn't street legal, so having access to wheels via Dante and Lewis was a plus.

One night, the guys picked me up at the law firm. We had our usual boardroom meeting to discuss the night's party, but I didn't know that Dante and Lewis had been on a robbing spree for the past couple of days. I got in the car with them, and we started our usual shit, hanging out, chasing women. It was a typical night until Dante and Lewis decided to drive to an area called Southgate.

Dante and Lewis had attitude problems. They'd gangbang on anyone they saw, without thinking of the consequences. There was a guy there, from a Southside gang, the East Coast Crips. I didn't know him, but Dante did. He started an argument with the guy. After the gangbanger walked off, Dante turned around and robbed an innocent bystander just for the hell of it. I was in the truck, looking at Dante, thinking, "What an idiot. We're in the middle of the fucking street. Why would he rob someone in the wide open like that?" Next thing I knew, the gangbanger had come back with his crew. Ten of them. Dante was so busy beating the bystander, he didn't even notice.

There were five of us: me, Dante, Lewis, Bernard, and T.J. We were outnumbered two to one. We got into it. Right there, in the middle of the street. Dante drove a green, old-style Chevy truck with a mattress in the bed, and it was loaded full of guns. That was how we always rolled. Next thing you know, one of the Crips pulls out his gun. They did not realize our firepower. I was standing on the bumper and when they started shooting, I jumped and hit that mattress and grabbed my guns. We shot back. It was just *bang-bang-bang-bang-bang*.

I don't know how many shots were fired. I had three guns. I was shooting a .25, a .32, and a .22. It seemed like an eternity passed.

The Highway Patrol just happened to be driving down the street when they heard the shots fired. They hadn't been called. What the hell the Highway Patrol was doing on a side street, I don't know, but here they came. Bernard and Dante took off on foot, but T.J. and Lewis jumped in the truck and we took off in a high-speed chase. They clocked us at 110 miles per hour. I was being bounced around the back of the pickup truck like a fucking Ping-Pong ball. The Highway Patrol called in reinforcements, and then we were being chased by the LAPD and the County Sheriff's Department. I couldn't see nothing at all. I couldn't get a grip on nothing. I was being tossed back and forth, but nobody was shooting at us, so I thought we might have a chance. Until we crashed.

We hit something so hard, I went into a daze. Lewis and T.J. took off on foot, but I just laid there on that mattress trying to recover. Since I was lying down, the cops didn't see me. They took off after T.J. and Lewis. They just left me there in the back of the truck. When I realized I was all alone, I couldn't believe it. I was like, "Oh shit, really?" I climbed out of the truck and started calmly walking away. That's when I heard, "Hey, you! Stop!" I ran. The Highway Patrol started chasing me on foot. I was able to run around the corner and there was a three-foot-high wall in front of me. I jumped over it and fell into some hedges. I heard the police run toward me, and then stop. They couldn't figure out where I went. I heard them call in on their radios. They reported that they were on foot chasing a Little black male, dressed in all red. I waited until they had run off, then I climbed out from the hedges. I started walking calmly across the street. Here comes the sheriff. They flashed a light in my eyes. "Hey you, what are you doing?" I said, "I'm on my way home." They looked me over. I was dressed in all red and I was a Little Person, but I was white, not black. They let me go.

I went into a Mexican restaurant. The helicopters were circling, and I'll never forget the lady there at the register. She took one look at me and saw something was wrong. She was so kind. "You okay?" she spoke in broken English. I said, "Yeah, I just need to rest." She pointed to the video game room, so I gave her five dollars, and she gave me a whole bunch of quarters. I hid in the back room of that restaurant, playing video games. Cops were running everywhere, looking for me. Finally, everything cooled down, and the cops left the area. I thanked the lady and left the restaurant. There was a bus coming, so I jumped on. I didn't know where I was going but I knew I was in a shitload of trouble.

I rode the bus downtown, then transferred to another bus that took me to Dante's house. I needed to think, to find out if anyone knew anything. I was too afraid to go back to Mama Myrt's. I thought the cops might be looking for me there. Dante hadn't made it home. Everyone got caught but me. Dante called from jail. His sister told him I was there, and he told her to put me on the phone. He said, "Shorty, you gotta do something. They're talking about giving us the death chamber." Apparently, three guys had been hit during our shootout, and one of them was the innocent bystander Dante had robbed. He was in the hospital, in critical condition, and the cops were saying all kinds of shit to scare the crap out of Dante. I got off the phone and Dante's sick mom let me spend the night in his room. After I left the next day, she had a heart attack.

I called Mama Myrt and she told me to come home. She said, "We'll take you up to Uncle D.'s house in Atascadero. You need to get outta town until we find out what's happening." I walked out of Dante's house and got about a block from the school on the corner. The kids were on recess, spilling out onto the sidewalks, when all of a sudden, five or six cop cars came out of nowhere. Screeching wheels, sirens, guns drawn, screaming into a megaphone. Kids running. Cops everywhere. It was chaos. They treated me like I was the biggest, baddest motherfucker. Like I was six-foot-nine and carrying an arsenal of weapons. They slammed me into the ground. I yelled, "I'm not armed!" It didn't help. Officer Martinez—I can still see his face—cuffed me and threw me in the back of his squad car. He smirked. "Enjoy your last breath of fresh air, you little piece of shit."

■　■　■

They took me to the Southgate substation. When I walked in, all the cops were laughing at the guys who'd been part of the chase the night before. "You let this little fuck get away from you?" It embarrassed them so badly they got pissed off. One of the cops kicked me as hard as he could in retaliation.

They put me in the holding tank. It was freezing in there, with no toilet. Finally, they pulled me out and said, "Tell us your story."

I said, "I don't know what you're talking about." The cop interrogating me said, "Your friends told us everything. You were with these guys all day yesterday." Turns out Dante and Lewis had been robbing people for hours before they picked me up at Wells Fargo. Thank God, I had proof I'd been at work at the law firm until six o'clock. Swipe cards don't lie. The cops didn't believe me. They kept questioning me and threatening me with the death penalty. They'd recovered all the pistols: Lewis told them I'd thrown the guns from the back of the truck and he took them on a tour, showed them where they could find all the tossed evidence. The cops told me they had my fingerprints all over the weapons. I knew they were right. My fingerprints were all over those guns, but they hadn't even fingerprinted me at the station yet, so I also knew they had no proof. They were lying. I told them, "I don't have nothing else to say." I didn't ask for a lawyer. I didn't know I could.

I asked to call my sister Janet. I told her, "I'm in jail." She couldn't believe it, and she started crying. Of course, I lied about everything. I didn't wanna tell her the truth. I wanted to keep her out of it and I didn't want her to tell my parents, but I knew, eventually, they would find out. Janet drove in from Palmdale to check on me. When they found out she was my sister, the cops started messing with her mind. They told her I was gonna get the death penalty and made her cry. One of the cops pulled her aside and acted concerned. "Take a good look at your brother. This is the last time you'll see him alive." They were upsetting her to try to get information out of me. It was a mind game, those four days at the substation. They were working on me and I just kept saying, "I don't know nothing."

Mama Myrt came down and tried to post bail, but they hadn't set the bail yet, so they wouldn't let me go. I was more worried about Coco than I was about myself. Mama Myrt promised me Coco would be taken care of. Little Al was watching him, but if things dragged on, they'd take Coco to Uncle D.'s house in Atascadero. They held me over the Martin Luther King Jr. holiday weekend. The reality of my situation began to sink in. It'd been six months since I broke off my wedding to Liz. I wondered: If I had married her, would I have been arrested? There was no way to know.

I started having the same dream every night. In the dream, I'd wake up in my own bed, at Mama Myrt's house, look around, and see everyone there. I'd have this happy feeling and be so relieved. Then I'd really wake up, and be in the prison cell. Son of a bitch! Oh, I was so mad to wake up like that. The dream continued every night for the entire time I was in holding. It was a miserable way to sleep.

On Tuesday morning, I went to Southgate Municipal Court for my preliminary hearing. It was a media circus. During that time in the late '80s and early '90s, the murder rates in Los Angeles and cities like Philadelphia and Chicago were sky-high. Crack cocaine was around on a massive scale, and guys who did that shit were nuts. South Central had the worst crack problem in the country, and that meant violence. Gangs were on a killing spree. There was so much senseless killing, so many drive-bys. It was on the news every night. There was a spotlight of national media attention on the entire South Central community. Police estimated that there were seventy thousand active gangbangers in Los Angeles alone. The city was the Gang Capital of the World.

At the same time, everybody and their brother wanted to be glorified as a gang member. Gangster rap was all over MTV, kids were getting gang tattoos when they weren't even in gangs, the movie *Colors* came out, and even white kids in the suburbs were wearing baggy jeans around their knees, red bandanas on their heads, and gold grills across their teeth. It was like the more the media demonized South Central, the more everyone wanted to either pretend to be a part of it or join up. Gangs that had no juice suddenly had juice. New gangs formed.

There was a public outcry for the police and government to "do something," so politicians were promising to "crack down on crack" and "clean up the streets," or "gang up on gangs" or whatever stupid thing they could say about it. In Los Angeles, they were passing a Gang Act that essentially labeled anyone involved in a gang a "terrorist" against the city or the state, so they could enforce longer sentences and press for more serious charges in court.

That's what we were walking into that Tuesday, at our arraignment. Since there were five defendants, and one of them happened to be a midget, the press had a field day. The *L.A. Times,* the *L.A. Sentinel,* and the *Herald Examiner* all covered the story. We were profiled on the evening news. My mug shot was in the papers. The headlines read: "Four Foot Gunman Leader of a Black Gang." Leader of a gang? I was on the bottom of the totem pole and anyone who was in the Bloods knew that. But the press didn't. They made up what they wanted me to be. Or maybe some cop wanted his five minutes of fame and gave them his opinion of my position. Either way, it was all lies. Pure sensationalism that made for great copy. It got picked up by the newswires. My face was splashed all over the L.A. papers. It also ran in the Little People of America quarterly newsletter: "Shorty Rossi, the son of Sonny and Dixie Rossi, was arrested . . ." Blah, blah, blah. I could just imagine the horror on my dad's face.

We stood accused of heinous crimes, and 'cause there was a robbery in progress during the shooting, we were considered the instigators of the fight. I was charged with everything: four counts of attempted murder, four counts of attempted robbery, four counts of conspiracy to commit murder, and a whole list of gun charges. The public defender turned to me that day and said, "Shorty, they're trying to kill you." She explained to me that the conspiracy charges were a way to prove intent, like we had planned to commit murder, like we had planned the robbery, like we had planned the shoot-out. I had nothing to do with the robbery. I got in that car to pick up girls. I defended myself when the Crips started shooting, but unbelievably, my shots were the only ones that actually hit anyone. Out of fifteen gangbangers shooting God knows how many shots out of God knows how many guns, only my bullets landed. I hit two

of the gangbangers and had accidentally shot that poor innocent bystander that Dante was robbing. My attorney stood up
in my defense. "Your Honor, this is the first time Mr. Rossi has
ever been arrested." The judge just looked at me and said, "No,
this is just the first time he's been caught." It sunk in hard what
was going on. I was totally fucked.

Mom said she blamed herself. She was convinced that if
she'd stopped me from running away, none of this would have
happened. I had to tell her, "Do you know what I was doing in
junior high? I was smoking cigars. I was smoking marijuana.
I was drinking. I lost my virginity. You never knew none of
that. So how can you blame yourself when you didn't know
what your kids were doing?" She cried and said, "I should have
known." There was no way she could have known. I had lied to
her face every single day. I even lied about prom night. I went
and partied in South Central L.A. instead. Yeah, she could
have paid better attention to what I was doing, but I was a liar,
plain and simple. I'd gotten myself into this mess. I had no one
to blame but me.

They shipped me to Men's Central Jail, or what we called
County. County was a holding pen for all the guys standing
trial or awaiting sentencing. The biggest jail in the world, there
were thousands of guys there—all of us housed in downtown
L.A. near Union Station. They put me in the old Hall of Justice
'cause they didn't know what to do with me. They were worried I might get hurt 'cause of my size and my gang affiliation
as a Blood. They took me to the Young Tank, where they held
the kids. A few days later, they transferred me back to Men's

take a deal so I wouldn't have to go through the daily grind anymore. She didn't listen to me.

With each new trial, charges were dropped. The conspiracy charges and accessory charges fell away 'cause I could prove I was at work during those hours. But the attempted-murder charge against the innocent bystander was still standing. Out of the five of us that were arrested that night, I was the only one who faced a jury. Dante and Lewis ratted against me. They took deals to save their own asses. When they put T.J. and Bernard on the stand, they had nothing to say. Since they were juveniles, so they got a lot less time. As for the two Crips that were shot, they had, of course, not pressed charges against me, 'cause they had no intention of spending any more time in a courthouse, or with cops, than necessary. The only guy that showed up every day was the bystander. He was there for every session. He'd survived, but he had to wear a colostomy bag for the rest of his life. He wanted justice and I was the only one on trial.

Dante portrayed me as the boss. He gave the jury the impression that I'd told him to rob the bystander and had masterminded the shoot-out. Dante was over six feet tall and solid as a rock. Like I could force him to do anything. When they brought Dante into County, he said he was a Blood. But Dante wasn't actually a Blood. He ran with guys who were Bloods, but he'd just ratted on me in court, and word spread fast. When the deputies walked him into the Blood module, he got his ass beat. They had to get him out of there and put him back into "gen pop," general population.

Then the Crips devised a plan to get back at Dante for shooting at their guys. They convinced him to become a Crip, since the Bloods wanted nothing to do with him. They pretended to convert him, and he even got Crip tattoos on his arms. Once the deputies moved him into the Crip module, they ripped him apart. Dante showed up in court and accused me of putting a hit out on him. He thought I had something to do with it, but I didn't. I didn't have to say a word. Dante had dug his own grave.

His accusation alone made things harder on me in the eyes of the jury. I kept hoping they'd offer me a deal, but the prosecutor came back with outrageous numbers: forty years to life, thirty-five years to life. Then to make matters worse, I was accused of taking part in a foiled escape attempt.

We were being bused back to County on these really old, big, long yellow school buses that were fortified and converted for prisoner transport. Normally, I was seated up front, in the cages with Bloods, but for some reason, the deputies sat me in the back with the Mexican gangs. I was actually handcuffed to two Mexicans instead of to Bloods. During the ride, the Mexican gang started ripping out the backseat. I saw it happening, but none of the deputies up front noticed. Eventually, they ripped a hole big enough to bust out of the back of the bus. We were locked together in threes, so the three guys that had been ripping all disappeared out the hole. Then one of the guys chained to me decided to make a break for it. For a split second, I thought about it, but I knew it would only make matters worse. If the third guy chained to us had decided to bolt,

I'd have had no choice. I couldn't hold back two grown men, but thankfully, he didn't bolt. He stayed put, so our handcuffed third ended up halfway into the hole, unable to move. As soon as the escapees busted out of the back of the bus, there was a cop car behind them. The bus swerved over to the curb and cops swarmed in. They saw the guy connected to me halfway down the hole, and they charged us all with attempted escape.

They took me out of the gang module and put me in the high-security row with Richard Ramirez, the Night Stalker murderer, and Todd Bridges, who played Willis on *Diff'rent Strokes*. Ramirez was there 'cause he was a scary mother. Bridges was there 'cause celebrities are very rarely mainstreamed into gen pop. It's too dangerous for them. Todd Bridges was the biggest crybaby. He'd purposefully plug up his toilet and flood out the tier. It was hard for him, very hard for him, to be in jail.

Even though the gangbanger testified that I wouldn't jump out of the bus with him, I became known as an escape artist. From that point on, I had to wear handcuffs with chains around my waist, hanging down to my ankles, and chains around my ankles. 'Cause I was "pint-sized," the deputies were afraid I could "fit into anything," so they decided to keep me in a one-man cell for twenty-three hours a day for the next six months of my trial. Being in solitary for those six months made everything even harder. I had to get up earlier for trial and 'cause I was now labeled a "high-security risk," I had to be put in a cage by myself on the bus. With those chains around my ankles, it was hard for me even to get on the bus. I'd need a little bounce to hop up, or some guy would have to lift me. If an inmate lifted me up, it was better. The deputies would always make a joke out of it and piss me off.

Being on the high-security tier, I spent a lot more time alone, and had a lot less time outside my cell. It was depressing and a mind game. I had to find some way to occupy my thoughts. I started reading more and got a copy of Donald Trump's *The Art of the Deal.* Trump talked a lot about using negativity to motivate himself. I wondered if there was a way to use my surroundings, dismal as they were, and make them into a positive, motivating force for myself. I liked that Trump had an ego. He didn't mince words, and he wrote with such authority that I couldn't help but be impressed by him. He was bigger than life. He was a character. I could relate. I wanted to meet him and pick his brain.

His life was exactly the life I had dreamed for myself when I was a kid, selling mice to the pet stores and dressing up like J.R. for Halloween. The opening chapter of his book walked me through a typical week in the life of a mogul, and all the important people he'd talk with or meet. I could picture that life for myself. I wanted it. I memorized the eleven steps for success he outlined, from Thinking Big to Maximizing Options to Fighting Back to Delivering the Goods. His book started to feel like my bible.

I just wanted the third trial to be over and done with so I could get out of County and move on. Janet, Mama Myrt, and Cerisse attended most of the trials. It was hard to see all of them crying. Mom and Linda came once or twice, but Dad never showed his face. I'd have pleaded guilty to the accidental shooting of the bystander, but they wouldn't drop the other charges, and the prosecution was going full-court press. Carol told me if I pled guilty, they'd throw the maximum time at me and that letting a jury decide my fate was my best shot at going home before I was ninety. Carol didn't want me to testify in my own defense, but I wanted to clear my name about the things I hadn't done. I was being accused of a lot more than what actually happened on that night.

I got on the stand and Kevin McCormick, the prosecutor, asked me point-blank, "Did you ever gangbang?" I said, "No." Then he said, "Can you explain these photos?" He projected photos of me, in County with my homies, all of them gangbangers, all of us wearing our County blues and red bandanas, throwing up gang signs. He was good, that guy. I had to hand it to him.

The other prisoners told me, "If the jury comes back quick from deliberations, you're screwed. If they take several days, it might go to a hung jury" (which happened during my second trial), "and if they take a day or two, you've got a chance of an acquittal." My third jury went out and took forever. For four days, I sat in the holding tank for nine hours while they deliberated, had some lunch, and deliberated some more. There were so many charges still pending against me for the jury to consider. There were still twenty-one gun charges alone, not to mention the attempted-murder, robbery, and conspiracy charge for the shooting of the bystander. In total, I was facing life in prison.

When the jury came back, they started reading their

decision. I was found guilty of attempted murder and guilty of the attempted robbery. I was found guilty on a bunch of the gun allegations. But I was found not guilty of conspiracy and that was the big one. That charge came with an automatic twenty-five-years-to-life sentence. I was so relieved, I almost passed out. The bailiff came over and helped me sit down in my shackles. He heard me say, "Oh, thank God. I'm actually going home now." He thought I was crazy. He corrected me, "You're not going home today, sir." I looked up at him. "Yeah, but someday, I get to go home. No life sentence. No life." In some weird way, I was happy. When I got back to my cell, the Night Stalker, Richard Ramirez, congratulated me. "You were convicted, but you didn't get life."

Four weeks later, I took one last ride to the courthouse. The sentence hearing lasted six hours and I was sentenced to twenty years, eight months. That sounded pretty bad until I started doing the math in my head. I remembered Big Will's lesson about doing good time. I realized I'd be out in half that time. Actually, less than half. I'd already been in prison for nearly two years by the time my third trial was over. With the California Department of Corrections policy of one day off for one day served, I could be out in eight years or less.

As I was doing my mental calculations, I was shocked to hear Kevin McCormick actually advocate for me during sentencing. He stood up before the judge and said, "Mr. Rossi has a chance to correct his problems and learn from his mistakes. It's our recommendation he be housed in the California Youth Authority." I couldn't believe it. This guy, the guy who prosecuted me, was trying to help me out. I stared at him in awe and wondered why in the hell he'd just done that.

The judge agreed with him, and they gave me a second chance. Even though I was technically a California Department of Corrections commitment, they were gonna ship me to the California Youth Authority. The judge made it clear: "If you mess up one time, we send you straight to CDC. Got it?" I nodded. Got it.

4

Cat
Man

They shipped me to DeWitt Nelson in Stockton, California. The facility was named after a forestry official, and part of its rehabilitation programs included training juveniles to handle flooding in the San Joaquin Valley or to fight forest fires in the Sierras. All the Youth Authority lockups offered vocational training and psychological counseling services. Their mission was to reform kids, not just imprison them. We weren't even called inmates. We were called wards, and we were even allowed to wear our own clothes on the grounds.

There were four juvenile prisons near Stockton at that time. Karl Holton and O.H. Close were for high school–aged kids. DeWitt Nelson was for the college-aged kids, eighteen to twenty-five, and then there was N.A. Chaderjian, which was a max-security youth prison for the serious fuck-ups. Those were the violent kids that had to be isolated. To get sent to Chad, you had to stab somebody or rape somebody. You had to have mental problems, and if you screwed up too many times at any of the other three facilities, they'd send you to Chad.

Every youth prison had a school, which we called the Education Department, as well as a vocational training department, a kitchen program, and religious services. DeWitt had a bunch of other offerings, including a gym, a track, and a field for football and soccer. It functioned like a self-contained city. The grounds looked like a college campus, with trees and grass. We even lived dorm-style, in halls with long rows of beds instead of cells. There were eight dorms holding three hundred kids per dorm. Nobody was separated 'cause of race or gang affiliation. It may sound like going to college, but there was still violence at DeWitt. Every year, on some specific day, the northern Mexicans and the southern Mexicans would have a bloodbath. There was still some gang activity, but for the most part, kids tried to share a mutual understanding of each other. For some reason, it worked.

Lassen was the intake dorm, where new arrivals were housed and most of the kitchen workers lived. Tahoe was the fuck-up dorm, where they stuck the kids who had behavior problems. There were two other dorms for the California Department of Forestry kids, who were training to fight fires. They had a lot less time and were in a lot less trouble than the rest of us. There was no way I could physically keep up with the demands of the fire training program and they didn't see me doing yard work or working the kitchen detail, so I was housed inside both the Pumas and Klamath dorms during my stay. They were the "good" dorms, dorms for those focusing on their education or on vocational training. They were smaller dorms than the rest, with more privileges and rewards built in, like a TV in the dayroom.

The dorms themselves were basically wide-open wings with rows and rows of bunk beds. Each unit had a security office, an entertainment/dayroom, and then an A wing, a B wing, and a C wing of bunk beds. The floor plan was completely open. There was no restriction on movement from wing to wing, and there was absolutely no privacy. We kept our limited belongings in lockers.

If you screwed up once or twice, they'd throw you in a wet room. Every unit had a wet room, a small cell with a bed, a toilet, no windows, the lights on twenty-four hours a day, and a camera watching your every move behind a solid steel door. It was solitary confinement in the midst of a pretty social, lenient environment, which made it that much worse. To know your buddies were out there, shooting hoops or going to school, and you were stuck in the wet room was hell. If you caused real trouble, with a weapons-related altercation, a rape, a stabbing, or assaulting an officer or a teacher, they sent your ass immediately to Chad, and nobody wanted to end up at Chad, so everyone tried to avoid conflicts if at all possible.

After being in high-security lockup at County for six months, I felt lucky. At County, I was miserable. At DeWitt, I felt almost free, but it still took me six months to start acting right. I got into fights. I got into trouble. I got in an argument with a guy and he hit me in the head. I said, "Okay, I'll be back," and back I came with soap in a sock. I whacked him hard and knocked him out. They stuck me in the wet room for that one.

I didn't wanna talk about my crime. I used the excuse that I was "going through the appeals process," but really, I was being defiant and arrogant. I had anger problems and I couldn't control my temper. They kept sending me to a psychiatrist, and he finally just laid into me, "You're mentally competent. There's no problem in your head. You're not fooling anybody anymore. You can turn this around." I realized he was right. I wasn't a psycho. I'd made a huge mistake but I wasn't a Jeffrey Dahmer or a Richard Ramirez. I was just stubborn as a mule. And that was a choice.

It took an inmate named Pinnock to set me straight. He pulled me aside one day and said, "Shorty, you got a lot here. Don't fuck it up." Here I was, being given a second chance in a place where the corrections officers and counselors and teachers were actually there to help. The corrections officers were not as violent or racist or bigoted as the guys at County, and if they were, they kept it to themselves. They didn't treat me like shit, and they didn't have carte blanche either. I started to get it. If I could act like a civilized human being, I'd be treated better by the guards and by all the staff. I started to understand their notion of "being a product of my environment," and started to believe that maybe I didn't have to act like an asshole all the time. Maybe I could do something good.

I registered to finish my high school diploma, got my GED, and got a job as a teacher's aide in the Employability Skills class. I liked being a TA, so I did it again for the Construction class and the Vocational Program. I was well liked by the teachers in the Education Department, and I was seen as helpful. I took anger management courses and the victim awareness training program that was offered. The full weight of my actions began to register.

I thought a lot about that innocent bystander. It wasn't right, what I'd done. I felt bad for him. I'd said as much in court. But when I said those words in court, there was the incentive that it might get me out of doing longer time. I didn't lie, but I didn't really realize the extreme damage I'd done to that man and his family. It hit me hard, and I was determined never to do something that terrible again. My transformation in attitude earned me the trust of the corrections officers. They started to let me do whatever I wanted. They knew I wasn't selling drugs, and they knew I had no plans to escape.

I got a job as a law clerk in the legal library. By law, every inmate has to have access to legal information, so I'd set up meetings all day long to help inmates with their habeas corpus, their writs, their complaints, their grievances. I was working my ass off, but that's where I wanted to be. I had my own office with a TV and a computer. I was responsible for logging every book in and out, and I created a database system for tracking them, so that each book could easily be found and used. Computers were pretty new at that time, so I seemed like a total genius. It gave me a lot of freedom. I didn't have to stay in my dorm all the time. I could leave in the morning and not come back until late in the evening. Eventually, the guards let me have my dinner in my office and watch TV. That was a huge deal, to have access to privacy.

Janet had come to visit me a lot when I was in County, even though she was frantically scared to be there, but once she moved to Phoenix, I didn't get to see her much. She still sent letters and packages. Mama Myrt and her family came every now and again, but those visits slowly dissipated. If Mama Myrt visited every family member or friend in prison on a regular basis, she would have gotten nothing else done. Linda came with her husband and brought my niece and nephew. Mom came once and Dad even showed up for a surprise visit on a day when visitors weren't scheduled. He happened to be in Sacramento, I don't know why, and he decided he was just gonna "drop by" and say hello. The officer told me my dad was waiting to see me and I didn't believe him. I thought he was playing a trick on me. I wouldn't even go look until another guard came down and said, "No, Shorty, really, there's another Little Person up there. It's gotta be your dad."

When I finally believed them and walked out to see, there was Dad, standing there as if "dropping by" a prison unannounced, and on a day when no other visitors were allowed, was the most normal thing to do. We sat down, we talked about Mom and San Antonio and when I thought I might get out. It was civil. We didn't talk about the fact that we weren't really speaking; that he hadn't come to the trials, or visited me before. As long as we were sitting face-to-face, we just small talked like nothing was wrong, in denial. Acting like everything was okay. That's the way he chose to handle it. That was the extent of our relationship. What he said about me when he left, who knows. Behind my back, it was always blah, blah, and blah.

Being at DeWitt, I didn't really care what was going on out in the real world. It was nice to see people, hang out with them, play games, or have lunch, but you're in a room with everyone else that's having a visit, so it's loud and there's no real way to connect. Maybe if I got to see people on a more regular basis, I'd have liked it better, but the visits were few and far between. They seemed like more of a hassle than a reward.

Besides, DeWitt was my world, for now. It was too hard to hear about what was going on without me, outside. It was a distraction to get letters and phone calls and packages. I appreciated them when they came, but my focus was on doing good time and getting my sentence out of the way so I could move on and live a new and better life. I became more and more independent. After a few years, the visits dried completely up. That was okay with me. Seeing people could wait until I was out.

I found a new family at DeWitt—the feral cats that lived behind the Education Building. There were probably fifteen or twenty cats that hung out back there, though most were skittish, so I couldn't get an accurate count. I started saving part of my lunches and dinners to feed them, and when the cooks heard what I was doing, they made sure to load me up with extra food or save the leftovers for me. I became known as the Cat Man, and dinnertime at the library became a feeding frenzy. I thought by feeding them, I was helping them out, but I made a real mess of things. Now that they were well fed, they started breeding like crazy. More cats showed up, and we went from having fifteen or twenty cats to an overpopulation explosion. There were hundreds of cats and kittens hanging around. I'd created a real problem.

The warden of DeWitt, Mike Gallegos, came out to examine the situation. He said, "Shorty, there are more cats here than we've got students!" He was trying to figure out how to handle the mess, and someone on his staff suggested they poison them all. I was in an uproar and I mobilized the teachers and staff and even the other wards to protest that decision. Poisoning was off the table. So Mike made me an offer. He could call in the Humane Society, or I could trap the cats, one by one, and if they were healthy, they would be spayed or neutered, then they could be released on nearby farms to help control the rodent populations in the San Joaquin Valley. I didn't trust the Humane Society not to euthanize all the cats, so I agreed to trap them on one condition: I wanted to keep five of them as pets.

Deal.

I spent hours trying to catch the cats. I figured out they had two entryways into the yard, and I placed ten traps near those high-traffic areas. The traps were humane, small steel cages with food in the middle. The program was successful. The numbers were going steadily down. But there was one cat I called Thomas, who just wouldn't cooperate. He was a huge, gray tomcat, muscular and smart. He was scrappy, a fighter, and the biggest cat I'd ever seen in my life. He was a bad-ass son of a bitch. I respected him for that.

He watched me set the traps, and figured out that if he just whacked the traps with a good swipe of the paw, he could knock them over and get the food without getting caught. In the mornings, if I came out and found the traps turned over and empty, I knew Thomas had been hard at work. I decided to give up trying to catch Thomas. He could be one of my five "keepers"—I'd make Thomas a pet. Of course, the next day, Thomas was trapped. Before I knew what had happened, one of the guards who'd been helping with the cat rescue shipped him off to a local farm. I was really upset. Thomas may have been a bastard but I'd really started to like him.

A week or so later, Thomas sauntered in like he'd never left. He looked like hell. A dog or raccoon had roughed him up, but he was still alive, and somehow he found his way back, over miles and miles of land. That cinched it for me. Thomas got to stay, and eventually he even let me pet and hold him.

I built my remaining cats a sanctuary behind the Education Building, since that's where they liked to hang. I got Landscaping to fill in a dirt plot and some of the teachers in the vocational classes lent me tools and scrap wood. I built a small house for my new friends, and the vocational guys built a few birdhouses for me. I hung them so the birds could nest in nearby trees, just out of reach of the cats. I got water and food bowls and placed them around, so every cat could eat. Of course, when Thomas came to eat, they all ran away until he was finished. I even managed to get my hands on a hammock and I strung it up between two trees so I could come out, lie down, and let Zsa Zsa take a nap on my chest. Zsa Zsa was a pretty calico, and the best of them all. She was MY cat. I played favorites for sure.

That cat sanctuary was my oasis. With the birds twirping and the cats meowing, I could go out there, get away from the world, and breathe. The cats brought peace to my life. I felt like I was taking care of God's creatures. They didn't ask for much, except to be fed. They let me know when they were hungry. They liked a rub behind their ears and that's all they wanted— unlike humans, who need so much and can't be trusted. I'd get so relaxed in my oasis that a couple of times I fell asleep swinging back and forth in that hammock. The principal, a few of the corrections officers, and one teacher knew about the sanctuary. They called it Shorty's Cave. If I missed count, they knew where to find me, snoring. For the next two years at DeWitt, I managed the law library and the cat rescue program, and happily swung in my hammock on sunny days.

DeWitt turned out to be the best place for me. I could look around and see I was helping these cats, helping other inmates, and even helping the teachers do a better job. I could use my talents to make a positive change in my community. Those last two years in the Nickerson Gardens projects had been total chaos. Now I understood that I could use my intelligence in a good way. Instead of being a negative manipulator, I could be a positive manipulator. I'd always had an authoritative type of personality, but I'd never been allowed to be in charge in a good way.

DeWitt straightened me up. I had no choice about being there, so why wouldn't I try to make the best out of that situation? There were other inmates who were miserable, but I just saw them choosing to make their lives more difficult. They complained. They made trouble. They spent all their time in the wet room. A very small percentage killed themselves 'cause they couldn't deal. I tried to make the best out of the circumstances I was in. What else could I do? I was gonna be there for years. I had to find a way to enjoy life.

I was at DeWitt from August 1989 to January 1993, and in those four years, I became a different person. The teachers and the guards around me were strong influences. There was a teacher named Sonya Miller, who looked beyond what'd I'd done and accepted me for who I was as a person. Jones Moore, my counselor, helped guide me through the courses, and though most of the other kids hated him, I liked him a lot. He was a big black guy who didn't care what anyone thought about him, in sort of an arrogant way, just like me. The corrections officers, Don Reynolds and Larry Mackey, gave me the opportunity to act right and rewarded me with extra privileges. Don and I got close 'cause he was the guard at the school where my office was located. We'd watch TV together, or play video golf on the computer. He was a big influence on me. He treated me like a human. Vic Federico, the principal, believed in me, and Mike, the warden, trusted me to run the cat rescue program. They were people who believed in second chances and in helping kids out. They knew if they invested in me, I wouldn't get back on that road. I am who I am today 'cause of their belief in me.

That's why my transfer came as such a shock.

5

Folsom

Twenty-five. That's the magic number in the California penal system. Twenty-five and you're an adult. Twenty-five and your ass is headed to a big house. No more Youth Authority. No more juvie treatment. Twenty-five was the end of the road. In 1993, when I turned twenty-four, I knew I had one year left before they handed me over to the California Department of Corrections. I was state property, and the state was gonna take me whether I liked it or not. They could stick me anywhere. I decided to head them off at the pass. I applied for clemency. I'd done good time at the Youth Authority. I stayed out of trouble, no fights. I showed up for my job every day. I got my GED and a degree in paralegal studies. I sat through anger management classes and victim awareness training, plus all the work I'd done on behalf of my cats. I had plenty of proof I'd gone above and beyond the definition of good time. There was no reason not to try.

I called up Carol, my trial attorney, and had her help me

petition the court. I got the backing of the warden and the assistant warden. I asked for letters of support from the director of the Youth Authority, and my application even went to the director of the California Department of Corrections. He allowed it to move forward. I even reached out to Kevin McCormick, the district attorney who prosecuted me. He had no objections. Everything was looking good. My application was going all the way to Governor Pete Wilson. For about eight months, I waited to hear. Then, about four months before my twenty-fifth birthday, Jones, my counselor, sat me down and just gave it to me straight. He said, "Shorty, I don't know how to tell you this, but they denied your clemency based on the violent nature of your crimes." It was like he'd just punched me in the stomach.

Pete Wilson basically gave me the finger. He didn't care that I'd finished high school behind bars. He didn't care that I'd been running my own version of an animal rescue operation on the grounds. There was no way he was gonna sign those clemency papers, even if I was an actual angel sent from heaven to walk the earth. He was turning down guys who should not have been there in the first place. Guys who'd been caught with minuscule amounts of drugs. Other inmates had screwed shit up. They'd let some other idiot out and he did something stupid and fucked it up for everybody else. Namely me. All that good work was just considered gone. My spirit was defeated.

With the clemency option off the table, Carol petitioned to get me transferred into the federal system. There was a federal prison called Lompoc, near Santa Barbara. Lompoc was a country club. It even had a golf course, plus there was a chance the Feds would let me out earlier if I could get transferred into their custody. No such luck. They shot that idea down, and two months before I turned twenty-five, they shackled my wrists and legs to my waist, loaded me up, and sent me to DVI, the Deuel Vocational Institution in Tracy, California. DVI was a purgatory, a reception center for newly committed prisoners or transfers, that had a long-standing reputation for being dangerous. There were so many fights they called it "Gladiator School."

DVI held thousands of guys being shipped all over the state. I knew a handful of them from the neighborhood, or from doing time together, but we didn't see much of each other behind those walls. DVI didn't mix minor offenders with guys who were never going home. If a guy had seven months left on his sentence, and he did something stupid, he might not go home for another ten years. So the DVI policy was to keep murderers away from molesters, thieves away from rapists. Every guy was locked down in his own cell and fed through a slot. We got one hour a day to either shower or visit the dayroom. Once in a blue moon, we'd get sixty minutes of rec time. In that one measly hour we had to socialize, the topic of conversation was always, "Where will we end up?"

Every guy had his opinion, either from personal experience or from rumors. Mostly, I heard warnings: "You don't want Corcoran." "You don't wanna go to Pelican Bay." "Stay away from San Quentin." "You don't wanna end up in Folsom."

But I also got some good advice, like, "You gotta ask to see the counselors if you wanna get through processing faster." I don't remember who told me that, but they were right. No state worker was gonna move any faster than they had to. My transfer counselor didn't care if I was there for two weeks or another six months. If I wanted out, I'd have to take control of my own "therapy," and believe me, I wanted out. DVI was hell, and the time I did there only counted toward my time served, it didn't count day-for-day. Waiting around at DVI was the equivalent of doing bad time. Useless.

The psychiatrists and counselors held the next five to ten years of my life in their hands. They were the ones deciding where to put me, and the ones tallying up my points. My "points" were based on the length of my sentence, the nature of my crime, and how much good time I'd done. By now, my points were low. I was considered a Level One or Level Two at most, and Level One was model behavior. That meant I had the right to be housed in the lowest-security facilities. It meant I could avoid doing time in a Level Four, the most dangerous prisons, filled with gang guys, child molesters, snitches, flight risks, and high-profile cases. I was a Level One and that was a good thing. It meant I had some options.

I didn't wanna be anywhere near Los Angeles. The Southern California prisons were full of Bloods, and I knew I had to get away if I wanted to stay out of trouble. I picked my first choice: Vacaville, in Solano County. The prison there was called CMF, the California Medical Facility, 'cause there was a huge hospital on the grounds. They had open dormitories, and a lot more freedom. My backup choice was the Avenal State Prison in Kings County, 'cause they had open dorms and seven hundred acres of land. Both prisons offered college courses, which I wanted to take, and they had easier, less violent reputations. I made my picks, and then, like the three thousand other guys sitting at Deuel, I waited. It was like gambling. You made a shot for it, but you never knew what was gonna happen.

They had five days before my birthday or five days after my birthday to transfer me. They wouldn't give any inmate the exact date of transfer, to keep guys from arranging escapes. So two days before my birthday, they woke me up, yelling, "Okay, pack it up, Shorty. You're moving!" They marched me into R&R (receiving and release), and that's when they told me I was shipping to Folsom. At first, I thought I heard them wrong, but as the news settled in, I went from confused to goddamn pissed. I screamed at the officer, "Folsom! What the fuck did I do?"

Folsom State Prison was going from bad to worse. Folsom was four thousand guys locked up behind sixteen-foot-high walls that were four feet thick. Folsom was Level Four gang territory. Folsom had bloody and violent riots. Folsom was the end of the line. I started screaming, "My points are low. I'm a Level One! Folsom is maximum security!" I threw such a fit, the officers had to get my counselor. First, he tried to convince me that Folsom wasn't that bad. He explained there was a minimum-security unit within the compound, despite the fact that the prison itself was a Level Four. I wasn't buying it and I wasn't budging. Then he just had to come clean about what had really happened.

The system still considered me a flight risk 'cause of my height. They thought I could stow away in a breadbasket or something. My counselor invoked the "bus situation" as proof and that just boiled my blood. I blew a goddamn gasket. "For six years, I've said the same thing! I wasn't involved! The fucking hole was right under my feet! If I was gonna go, I'd have gone then! I can't run for shit anyway! Look at these legs!" I was never gonna live down that Mexican gang bus escape from County. Fifty guys on the bus and I got chained to those stupid idiots. My counselor just shrugged. I could scream until I was hoarse. They were shipping me to Folsom. There was nothing I could do.

They came to get me in the morning. The guards shackled my wrists together, my legs together, and then secured them both to a chain that circled my waist then dropped to my toes. I was belligerent. "Really? My wrists and my ankles? That's necessary?" The guard snorted, "You Little People are quick on your feet." I glared at him. "How many Little People are you dealing with on a daily basis?" The guard's neck turned red with anger. I pressed him. "How exactly do you have this information that Little People are quick on their feet?" The guard clamped the handcuffs tighter. Me and my stupid mouth. Now I couldn't even lift my leg to get on the bus. The guard realized he had to pick me up. Him putting his hands on me "to help" was fucking humiliating. We didn't even know each other, but he hated me and I hated him. He basically threw me onto the

with a lot less violence. But then Cinturino went one step too far. "We're gonna put you into a cell for the first week by yourself." Being alone in my cell was bad news. If I was asleep, and the cell opened up, someone could just slide in there and take me out. I insisted they put me in a cell with somebody I knew. The gang leaders decided my first cellie would be a young kid named J.D., the son of a guy I knew from the projects. Out of five thousand inmates, I'd be the only inmate in an interracial cell. Even the old guards, who'd been there for over twenty years, had never seen anyone do what I did. They thought I was crazy.

The day of my move, I felt fairly certain I was gonna die. If not, I'd at least be shanked, and I imagined it would be painful, but there was nothing I could do to protect myself. I'd never felt more powerless. Who knew whether the guards were really gonna guard me? They could have been Nazi sympathizers for all I knew. When they came to get me, I just took a deep breath and tried to look calm. I felt like I was walking to the chair. We made it out of Three Building with no problems, but once I set foot in Four Building, the Aryan Brotherhood made their move. A big-ass white motherfucker came charging at me. I don't know what he was thinking—there were guards all around me. Maybe he was trying to prove himself, but the guards saw him charge, and they slammed him to the ground about three feet away from me. I saw the knife in his hand, and that's about all I saw, 'cause suddenly, the guards swarmed from every direction. The place went into complete chaos. A guard pushed me into my cell, and then, slam, slam,

slam—cell doors started closing one by one. They put the whole prison on lockdown. J.D. and I stood inside the cell, just staring through the bars, as the guards dragged the guy away and the screaming, the banging, the noise was earsplitting. My stomach was in knots, but I wasn't dead. J.D. stared at me, eyes wide open. "Man, that was close."

Now, outside people assume that inmates are being stabbed or killed all the time, but those were the days of the late '70s and early '80s. Prisons had become a lot less violent since they'd instituted the SHU, the Security Housing Unit. It was a system they used to control the really nasty guys, the Hannibal Lecters of the world. Getting thrown into the SHU was essentially like being thrown in the wet room at the Youth Authority. It was solitary confinement for twenty-three hours a day. Things still happened, of course, just not as often, and in Four Building, it was even rarer. That's why the attempt on my life was met with such stiff and immediate punishment . . . lockdown. For the next week, nothing happened. Everybody was locked in their cells. We were let out once every other day to take a shower. Sleeping in my bunk those first few nights, I didn't feel safe. I trusted my cellie, but he was only one person, and lockdown in a prison is like a woman and her husband driving around skid row at three in the morning. She may trust her husband, and her doors may be locked, but she still wants the hell out of the 'hood.

Lockdown caused even more friction. The inmates were pissed and blaming me. Everyone wanted me shipped away or taken out. The officials convened another meeting with all the prison gang leaders to calm things down. Of course, the leaders lied and called a "truce" to lift the lockdown, but I knew that with the gates wide open, I was in serious jeopardy. Now anybody could get to me. Every time the guards opened our cells, the Bloods would show up to surround and walk with me. That woman driving around skid row would be a lot safer with three patrol cars escorting her home. The Bloods knew I'd stay alive a lot longer with three or four guys beside me at all times. There was a concerted effort to protect me. They were my patrol cars.

For my first walk across the yard, it took an entourage. I felt like a movie star, everybody staring at me. Crossing that yard was a crash course in Folsom's gangs and their turf. There was the Mexican Mafia, which was the oldest gang in California's system. They were considered a prison gang, not a street gang, 'cause they'd actually started at Deuel, the DVI prison I'd just left, and had been around for about forty years. Their members were mostly from Southern California. Across the yard from them was Nuestra Familia, another Latino gang that started at Soledad Prison in the 1960s but also had a strong presence on the street. They were made up of all the Northern Californian Mexicans, and they hated the Mexican Mafia. Then there were the Border Brothers, also Mexicans, to round out all the Hispanic gangs. As for the whites in the yard, there were two gangs that claimed space: the Aryan Brotherhood and the Nazi Low Riders, an Aryan Brotherhood spin-off that started at the Youth Authority back in the '70s. The Aryans were the ones that really hated me, though the Nazis had no love for me either. At County, I was used to the Bloods having one side of the yard and the Crips having the other, but at Folsom, all the black gangs shared turf—even the Black Guerrilla Family, which was another prison-not-street gang that had started in San Quentin. There weren't as many of them as there were Crips or Bloods, but they were still a presence.

Basically the yard was a bigger, more dangerous version of high school. The gangs almost functioned like self-contained cliques with their own "jocks" and "nerds" and "druggies" and, of course, the "popular" guys, the guys in charge, leaders who got their ass kissed by everybody. You could see them, giving orders with a slight nod or just a look. They ran the entire prison, and just like high school, most of them never wanted to leave. Once they got out of those walls, nobody would listen to them. On the yard, they were big men. Outside, they were nothing, nobody.

What shocked the shit out of me was seeing so many guys I knew from the projects. There were more Bloods in that yard than there were on the streets. It was like a damn reunion. I didn't know it then, but over the next five years, I came to realize prison was a never-ending cycle. If we ever got down to three or four Bloods in the building, ten more would get transferred in. It was just endless.

I saw cons come back through those bars five, six, seven times. They'd be let out on parole and three months later, they'd be back. They didn't have the motivation to succeed. Either they didn't care or they didn't know how to change their lives. It was too easy to do the same old things once they were out. Most of them went home to the exact spot where they got in trouble, and the temptation of the easy life was just too great. They'd think, "Why am I gonna be yelled at by this damn man, making seven dollars an hour, when I can be my own boss making seven dollars a minute?" Most guys didn't have the attention span to stick with the struggle. Not only were they a failure at being a gang member, they were a failure at school, a failure at home. They'd never had any success, so they didn't even know what it felt like to be someone different.

The only guys who didn't come back were those that wanted to be educated. They were the only ones that gave me any hope. The rest of the guys became institutionalized. There were guys who opted to stay in prison rather than deal with parole. They'd willingly do their full sentences so they wouldn't have to face the real world. Then there were the guys who'd go back out on the streets and get on parole, but they couldn't make it. They were starving. They had to hustle for everything. Then they'd have that one thought: "Why don't I go back to jail? It's easier there." We'd see them again. Jail became their comfort zone. Jail was all they knew. They didn't like change. They didn't like struggling, and in jail, they got fed three meals, the rules were clear, they had a job, and everything was structured, predictable. They always had someplace to sleep, a couple of girls on the side, and instant camaraderie. Jail was actually easier than having to be responsible for your own life. There were a lot of guys who just threw up their hands and surrendered.

It was the last thing I wanted to happen to me, but Folsom

functioned like a warehouse. The system wasn't focused on reform. It was focused on trying to keep people alive, controlled, and with minimal violence during the day. My cat sanctuary at DeWitt seemed a million miles away. Those easy moments in the hammock, with Zsa Zsa on my stomach, both of us asleep, those were long gone.

There was nothing for me to accomplish at Folsom. They offered high school programs but I'd already finished my GED. I asked to work for the PIA, the prison industry authority, (where they make all the state license plates), but the factory was in a different section of the building. To get to it, you had to cross eight different security perimeters, and prison officials still had some note on some damn piece of paper that said, "Flight Risk." They would not let me leave my unit to work.

There were guys in Folsom doing life, who had no chance of ever setting foot on free ground, and they'd let them work PIA, but not me. By now, I knew I only had about five years left on my sentence if I did good time and I certainly wasn't gonna do nothing to extend my stay. Once I was turned down for a PIA job, I felt hopeless. I couldn't take a step without an entourage of black asses in my face. I couldn't work a job to kill the time. I couldn't take the limited classes that were offered. I gave up on the system. There was no way to create meaning for myself, so I settled for making myself comfortable instead. I surrendered to the monotonous routine of prison life: meals, count, sleep, meals, count, sleep.

Breakfast was served at 6:30 in the morning. It was usually SOS, shit on a shingle, or gravy on a piece of meat. Some days, they served hotcakes or French toast, but I couldn't stand nothing with syrup on it. Thank God, they didn't force you to go. I hated getting up that early, so I mostly opted to sleep in until 8 a.m. and make instant coffee or Top Ramen noodles with my stinger, a slim metal rod that plugged into the wall, heated up, and brought water to a boil. Microwaves and hot plates were illegal. Stingers were the only option. You could buy them through the canteen, which was the commissary, but they'd run you about fifteen dollars. When guys couldn't afford to buy one, they'd take two square pieces of metal, put a piece of rubber in between them, and screw those together. They'd then attach a positive and a negative wire that they soldered onto the metal. It would get rusted and be dangerous. Guys would get zapped. End up in the hospital. Not everybody was bright enough to be messing with electricity.

Meals were the equivalent of herding cattle. It took two or three hours to feed everybody in a constant flow, an assembly line of guys coming and going all the time. You only had five or six minutes to eat. Once the guards said you were done, you were done, whether or not you still had food on your plate. Breakfast and dinnertime ran this way. Lunch was bagged. They'd slap some form of meat between two pieces of bread, toss in a piece of fruit, juice or milk, and maybe a small bag of potato chips. Lunch was meant to be carried with you to your job. Not that I had one.

There were few meals that were worth the trouble. Hamburgers I liked, but most of the time, I went to chow hall just for the ice cream. I wouldn't touch the rest of the food. I lived off junk food from the commissary: canned chili, canned tuna, canned oysters, Top Ramen noodles, potato chips, and popcorn. Money got to me through friends or family on the outside. Janet, Uncle D., who was back out of prison, and my roll dog from the projects, Jerry, would send me a quarterly package when he was out of jail. Quarterly packages were like care packages kids get sent at camp. We were allowed a set amount of stuff per package, so many Ramen noodles, so many cigarettes and cigars. Most of my quarterly packages were made up of cigars. Other than that, I smoked Swisher Sweets, 'cause that's what they sold at the commissary.

For those guys who didn't have friends or family sending them things, there were actually companies they could pay to send them a quarterly package. The companies mailed magazines or catalogs to inmates. Their entire customer base was in prison, and they were making millions. They sold radios, Walkmans, or TVs. They had setups with the prisons to actually debit inmates' prison accounts, so we never even had to write them a check or arrange for our family to do so. There was a whole industry that catered only to inmates. It was disturbing, but as long as there is a dollar bill flying around, somebody will grab it.

Since at first I wasn't able to have a job, I had to rely on gifts from somebody on the outside. Janet or Jerry or Uncle D. would send me somewhere between $20 and $200, and if I budgeted right, I'd only spend about $50 at the commissary every month. I could make those gifts last. It's not like having a job would have made me rich. Prison jobs only paid ten cents or fifteen cents an hour. At the max, guys made fifty cents an hour at their job. So a $15 stinger, which doesn't seem like a lot of money, was actually very expensive. Cigarettes were better than all the money in the world. You could always wheel and deal and negotiate if you had cigarettes. (I have no idea what those guys are doing, now that they've banned cigarettes in the prisons. I have no idea how they function. It would be like waking up tomorrow and finding out that there is no more cash in the world.)

You had to bribe the guys in the laundry to make sure you got your own stuff back. Everyone was issued a set of clothes. Our uniform was white T-shirts, white boxers, white socks, and PIA jeans and jean shirts, both of which were actually sewn by prisoners. Everybody had a jacket 'cause it did get cold. That was your basic. You had two or three of each piece, and each cell had metal compartment-like shelves with four different sections to split with your cellie. That's where you stored your stuff. Most guys had cardboard boxes slid underneath their bunks for extra storage, but if you were lucky, you could snatch a milk crate from the kitchen. I had five of those. Those were luxury, and illegal. Every couple of days, you'd trade your dirty laundry for clean basics. Sometimes, you would get crappy stuff back instead of your own clothes.

Since I am Little, I was allowed to have outside people send me special things. Janet would send me Levi's jeans and I'd have the guys in the sewing shop cut them down to size. For the price of a few packs, of course. Janet had to send me T-shirts and shoes 'cause they don't make prison shoes that small. So everything I owned was from the streets, and not from prison. I never wanted to lose my things, so I always made sure I paid someone to wash them personally.

Every transaction, every move I made, had to be thought out. How will I get my clothes back? How will I get the best bed? Who will be my cellie? When the new mattresses arrived, the desk clerk, an inmate, was in charge of handing them out. Now, those mattresses get old fast and they're only so thick to begin with. Most guys had two or three mattresses stacked on top of each other, but when the new ones came in the door, those were the ones in demand. There were five hundred beds and only two hundred new mattresses. Everything had a price.

The corrections officers just looked the other way. Maybe some didn't know what was going on, but most just turned a blind eye. There were certainly crooked corrections officers who had their hands in drugs, but they weren't gonna lose their pensions over a mattress or laundry.

At 4:30 p.m., no matter where we were, we had to head back to our cells for count. Count is a statewide activity. Every inmate in every prison in California goes into lockdown every single day at 4:30 p.m. You can set your watch by it. The corrections officers go cell to cell and literally count to see if anyone is missing. In Four Building, it was a process that normally took half an hour, but you'd be surprised at the uneducated people trying to do math. Four or five times a month, some stupid guard couldn't count past two hundred, and we'd all have to sit for two hours, even though no one was actually missing.

In the bigger buildings, count took much longer. One building was five stories high and held over three thousand prisoners. They had thirty or forty officers patrolling their tiers at any given time. Four Building had twelve guards, or less, walking the tiers. Our officers were around so much we knew them all by name. I was very clear on who liked me and who didn't. Half of the officers didn't like me 'cause I had a smart-ass mouth.

Sometimes, on a Sunday night, a group of guys would grab a table and cover it with Saran Wrap. We'd use our stingers to cook noodles and chili, then crush bags of potato chips and dump everything onto the table, cover it with mayonnaise and mustard, and mix that slop together. That was a community dinner with your friends. It was called the spread.

We'd all gather around and watch *Unsolved Mysteries*. Every so often, we'd see one of our guys profiled. One night, we were watching, and this old dude, a white guy, comes up on the screen. He had chopped up his girlfriend and put her in an ice chest. That guy lived six cells away from me. He'd been locked up so long, none of us knew why he was even there. He was a model inmate, and 'cause he was housed in Four Building, we all assumed he couldn't be that bad a guy. But cutting up a woman and putting her into an ice chest and storing her in a freezer for five years . . . that seemed pretty bad to me. The next time I walked past his cell, I looked at him very differently. "You still got that freezer?" He didn't even flinch, but said, "They aired it again, huh?" I guess he'd seen his story on *Unsolved Mysteries* before. Despite what he'd done, he struck me as a guy who would never do nothing wrong again. Of course, he'd never get that chance. He was in for life.

■ ■ ■

With nothing but time on my hands, I was devouring books. I checked out a copy of *My Autobiography* by Charlie Chaplin, and I became his biggest fan. Reading about his rough childhood, his alcoholic dad, his crazy mother, how broke he'd been as a kid. That he went on to become such a huge, international superstar only to be exiled. Man, Charlie had lived. He brought entertainment and laughter to everyone, all over the world.

I was so impressed by the fact that he'd cofounded United Artists, a film distribution company, with Mary Pickford, Douglas Fairbanks, and D. W. Griffith. They were actors, and they wanted more control over their careers and their projects. They took the power away from the old Hollywood system. Charlie even built his own studio. He was totally independent at a time when all the other actors were owned. That took some balls.

I was blown away when I read that he was accused of "un-American activities" and was labeled a communist. And that J. Edgar Hoover instructed the FBI to keep extensive secret files on him, and eventually kicked him out of America. Well, kept him from reentering the country after he went to his own damn film premiere in London. This man, who was so loved and had basically been an ambassador for America 'cause of his movies, ended up exiled to Switzerland. It was so insulting it seemed unbelievable.

I'd never really looked up to anyone in my life, especially not an actor or celebrity, but I truly admired Chaplin. I respected that Charlie was a determined man. He was gonna get his way, no matter what. He had opinions that were controversial and he was punished for holding his views. His views started some shit. He was ostracized. He never listened to anyone else about how to be successful. I was inspired by his life. I did my best to get ahold of his movies if they made their way behind bars.

His book stuck with me. It changed my whole attitude, and reminded me how productive and useful I'd felt at the Youth Authority. I knew I had more to offer to the world, and I didn't have to sit behind bars, twiddling my thumbs for five years, just biding my time.

It didn't cross my mind to become an entertainer. Entertainment was Chaplin's business, but it wouldn't be mine. I just wanted to be successful. I was still determined to be a lawyer or a corporate guy, but I knew, if I actually wanted to accomplish something in life, I had to start making those changes now.

To plan who I was gonna become, I needed to know where I'd come from. My friend Tony and I were interested in our Italian heritage, in learning more about our culture, even the language. Tony was one of my few white friends in Folsom. He wasn't an Aryan or a Nazi—I never would have tolerated a racist—but it was still hard for us to be friends, since he had to run with the white guys, and I was technically still a Blood. I found out we could register for an independent study class and use it to research our family trees. What was my bloodline, and could it explain how I'd ended up where I was?

In order to even start a family tree, I needed to talk to family. Janet didn't know much. Linda and I weren't in touch anymore, and to complicate matters further, Dad had told all our relatives on both sides of the family that I was away on a secret mission for the CIA. He was so embarrassed by my imprisonment that he made up a covert midget operation for the USA. Like I was a fucking spy. Seemed to me, the most noticeable thing in a foreign country would be a midget running around wreaking havoc, but Dad's side of the family seemed to believe it. I'd never spent much time with them in the first place, and I was gone for so long. They had no way of knowing anything I was doing, except what they heard out of Dad's mouth. Truth wasn't his specialty.

Then Janet called the prison and had them notify me that Nonnie died. I was devastated to hear about Nonnie. I loved her. Not being able to go to her funeral was a crushing loss. She was my family. I was still resentful about Mom and Dad putting her in a home. She'd been so good to me. I had to write about how wonderful this Little woman was to me. So I typed up her eulogy and Fed-Exed it to my great-aunt Wanda, who was handling the funeral arrangements. In prison, when you send something by Federal Express, you can't fill nothing out on the address label. You just give the mailroom a voucher, and they fill it out with a return shipping label from Folsom Prison. Needless to say, my aunt figured out I wasn't working for the CIA, but she kept her mouth shut. When the priest read the part of my letter that said, "Things are out of my hands, and I'm sorry I cannot be there," I imagine she made sure not to look at Dad.

Aunt Wanda was another woman I dearly loved, so now that she knew the truth, I reached out to her and asked questions I wasn't supposed to ask. I wrote to other long-lost relatives, and the letters that came back . . . they let some things slip. It was Wanda who first leaked the truth. She told me about my paternal granddad. That he hadn't been dead for my entire childhood. That he had, in fact, only died recently. She also told me he'd been locked up for domestic abuse. He must have been a brutal, vicious, violent man, 'cause back then, no Texas husband ever got locked away for beating his wife. Wife-beating was basically considered a privilege of marriage in those days. Then a cousin told me that my great-grandfather had been arrested in New York more than once. He didn't know the charges. Then, the big bomb dropped. I got a letter back that said, "Well, your dad was arrested too."

Wait? What? Dad was arrested? For what? When? Did he serve time? What jail? Nobody seemed to know the details, and I sure as hell couldn't call Mom up and ask her. I thought back and realized that Dad's arrest may have had something to do with his trouble at Lockheed. Something so bad had happened that he was fired. He had to go to court, and he'd done that community service in the park, but after that, we'd moved to Texas and I'd run away and never found out what had really happened. Linda and Janet were already out of the house, so they didn't know, and Mom and Dad never said nothing about Lockheed again.

So there it was. Turns out, I was a fourth-generation jail-bird. All the men in Dad's family had been arrested. Me, Dad, my grandfather, and my great-grandfather. Had I heard a word about this when I was a kid? Hell, no. Had Dad bothered to mention it when I was arrested? No, again. Another family secret. This was my history. I was just carrying on the family fucking tradition. My cousin laughed when I told him what I'd discovered. He said, "It may have been a tradition but you're the one who made it huge." My ancestors may have been in jail, but none of them had done ten years behind bars. I'd taken it to the next level. Unfortunately, the legacy didn't end with me. My nephews landed in jail too. For a night or two, nothing major, but still, it made me think about what it would take to stop the cycle. Maybe there's a Rossi temper, and we all just inherit it. Maybe it's the Rossi legacy to land in jail. Maybe it's a curse.

Researching Dad's side of the family and the history of beatings, abuse, and arrests was disheartening. It felt like fate had been in charge the whole time and I was just along for the ride. At least on Mom's branch of the tree there were entertainers, and nobody landed in jail. It gave me some hope that at least fifty percent of me had her genes. I didn't have to succumb to fate or genetics. I could choose another way.

It was as if by thinking those new thoughts, life shifted to test my resolve. Fate, the fickle bitch, presented me with an opportunity. She made me the Slumlord of Folsom.

6

Slumlord

By the time I got to Folsom, there were guys wearing "J" numbers and by wearing, I mean literally wearing. Physically, we wore our numbers on our clothes. These were numbers that were ours for the rest of our lives. They'd never be reassigned. If we ever ended up back in prison, we'd wear the same number. It was like having a Social Security card painted on your chest.

You could tell a lot about a guy by the letter in front of his numbers. The earlier his letter was in the alphabet, the longer he'd been behind bars, and the more respect that earned him. The letter was part of your street cred. The lower your letter, the higher the status. If a guy was wearing a "B" number, we could tell that he'd been in prison for at least twenty years. In all my years in the system, I only ever saw an "A" once. I wasn't sure whether to bow in front of the guy or feel sad for him.

I had some amount of cred 'cause I had an "E," and because of that—combined with the Legend of Shorty, and the nerve and the heart and the balls I had to put my life in jeopardy to live among the Bloods—the threats on my life began to subside. The Crips ignored me entirely. I'd managed to survive as a white Blood at Nickerson, at County, and at DeWitt, so they decided just to let me be. Outside the prison, they would've been my enemies, but inside they became my allies. The only guys still holding a grudge against me were the Aryans, and after a few more failed stabbing attempts, they finally just gave up. Guys weren't friendly, but they weren't hostile anymore, and after six months, the warden felt like it was safe enough to put me in the desk clerk job, answering phones. It was mindless work, nothing like getting to TA for the classes at DeWitt, and not even close to running the cat rescue program, but it was good to have some place to be for eight hours a day.

Once I had more freedom to move around, go to work, and meet people, I started making friends across all the color lines. Everybody got to know me 'cause I'm a pretty likable person, which I know is hard to believe 'cause of my TV persona, but it's true. I will have a conversation with anybody. I get along with all kinds of different people. I respect everybody until they give me a good reason not to. In prison, I changed guys' minds. "That son of a bitch who came in here was supposed to be the most evil bastard, but he turned out to be a likable little fuck."

I got along with my cellie, J.D., okay. When you shove two people into a tiny room, you are bound to get on each other's nerves, but we managed. Then J.D. was released, and I had to get a new cellie. I had a friend in another building who wanted to move to Four Building, but he wasn't allowed to come over because of his job. I was worried they were gonna stick me with some idiot, and I knew for sure they weren't gonna leave me the space to myself. I wanted to be able to control who moved in.

I'd become friends with a guy named Ray, even though he was from San Francisco and he wasn't a Blood. He was Fillmore Street Mob. In San Francisco, at that time, there weren't big gangs like the Bloods and Crips. It was divided up by smaller territories of where people were from. Guys identified themselves as Potrero Hill Projects or Hunters Point or Fillmore. They weren't into the gang signs and colors the way the gangs in L.A. were. All those guys ran with the Bay Area crew. That group included guys from San Francisco, San Mateo, Valeo, Oakland . . . Within that group, there were the smaller divisions of neighborhoods. We called them the 415 Guys. The 415 Guys were friends of the Bloods if something happened, and some guys mingled, but mostly the 415 Guys stayed on their side of the yard and we stayed on ours.

Ray and I didn't know each other very well. The cell beside me held a guy named O'Dell, and he and Ray were friends. Ray spent a lot of time outside my cell, and we got to be friendly. He didn't like his cellie, and he wanted to move, so when J.D. vacated the top bunk, Ray asked to be moved in.

This wasn't business as usual at Folsom. Ray and I were from different gangs, and the officers considered our living together a safety concern. But Ray was okay by me, and eventually, we convinced them it would be fine. It was only supposed to be a temporary solution until they could find more "appropriate" housing for both of us.

When you're in a room that's six feet by nine feet and you can totally ignore each other, that's a good cellie. After dinner, we'd get back in our cell. Ray would take the top bunk. I'd hit the bottom bunk, and he'd turn on the TV, or I'd put on my headphones and we wouldn't speak a word. Some nights, we'd play card games or we'd take turns cooking with our stinger. We got along, and Ray ended up being my cellie for the next four years.

Our cross-color, cross-gang friendship was just another example of my ability to get along with all the gangs, all the races, and to move freely among them. The guards had never seen nothing like it, and neither had the inmates. It afforded me a level of respect that superseded gang affiliation and all the accepted rules. Maybe it was my size that protected me. Maybe it was the thing that made me most vulnerable to danger that actually kept me safe.

Whatever the reason, when Four Building's housing clerk got rolled up for drugs and thrown into the SHU, the warden promoted me to "slumlord." Everyone was shocked. Me included. There were only five slumlords in the entire prison. It was the most coveted job, second only to being the warden's assistant. Its only duty was to make sure all the beds were filled, orchestrating the moves between five different buildings and between cells, but that meant dealing with every gang, every officer, and every administrator at Folsom.

Slumlord jobs went only to the guys who had done a lot of time, or who had a lot of power, and I didn't qualify as either. I had an "E" number. There were plenty of guys wearing "B," "C," and "D" that stood in front of me, rank-and-file. There were gang leaders who'd been itching for that job for years and years. I'd barely been at Folsom for a year, and suddenly I was gonna be in charge of Four Building. It was an outrage.

But the warden was tired of the housing clerk position being used as a way to ferry in drugs. In prison, there was access to any drug you wanted. The drugs came in through the guards, or were smuggled through the visitor center. The idiots either swallowed them or crammed them up their ass. They were easier to get behind bars than they were on the street. Just ten times more expensive, and very often, the housing clerk or slumlord of each building controlled the flow of the merchandise. Pot and heroin were most common, but if you had a taste for something else, you could find it.

I'd basically grown up around drugs, and I'd been a frequent recreational marijuana smoker, but thankfully, I didn't have the addictive personality that a lot of my friends had. My cellie Ray struggled to stay sober; it was his greatest battle. But when you're fourteen and your dad lights up a crack pipe and hands it to you to smoke, addiction is probably gonna be an issue. Ray really never had a chance against it.

Even when I was smoking cigars or cigarettes or marijuana, there was always a time when I could stop. Especially pot. I started smoking cigars when I was in seventh grade, and I smoked them all through prison, but I was always too scared to try heroin after seeing what it did to guys. There were guys my same age that once they touched it could not stop. I was a dangerous man, but I wasn't a stupid one. When it came to drugs, it just seemed stupid.

My only weakness was pruno, prison-made alcohol. It was the worst-tasting stuff, but it did the job, especially if you hadn't been drinking for days, weeks, or months. The guys on the third floor made it 'cause they lived on a less-patrolled tier. They'd collect any type of fruit, like oranges, apples, bananas, or raisins, and then they would steal a yeast packet from the kitchen and some sugar, and let that ferment in their cells. In Four Building, if you got caught with pruno in your cell, you got kicked out, or even worse, the deputies would purposely pop open the container and pour it all over your crap. That would make a stinky mess.

If I had a drink of that stuff, *whooooo*. There were a few times I was schnockered to the point where I needed help down the stairs. The corrections officers would see me and tell Ray to put me to bed. I'd get too loud. It was my only vice, so the officers looked the other way, as long as I kept my mouth shut. The warden probably knew about my pruno weakness, too, but he also knew that I didn't use drugs and I didn't sell. He'd watched me navigate friendships and change the minds of even the Aryans about me. He thought I was the right man for the job. I wasn't so sure.

The day the warden offered it to me, I sat Ray down in our cell to talk it through. Taking the slumlord job was a real risk. It didn't officially pay more, but of course, it did in other ways. There were perks, from being able to control who lived where to having access to my own office, and the freedom to roam from building to building. But there were also some real minuses to consider. Gang leaders would be pissed 'cause they wanted the job instead. A lot of the older officers made it clear to the warden that I'd been spoiled too fast. They felt it was too easy for me. Giving me the slumlord job was like rewarding a troublemaker. I had stirred up a pile of shit, and somehow come out smelling like a rose. Ray agreed. He said, "You just got everyone off your back and now, you're gonna have to be careful again."

It just seemed stupid to turn down the opportunity. Here I was, my whole life, wanting to be in charge of a corporation, to run an organization, to be "the boss," and fate had just handed me a job that sure as hell looked an awful lot like boss practice. No, it wasn't a Fortune 500 company, but it wasn't that far off from being in real estate . . . and good old Donald Trump had done pretty well in real estate. Every business has a hustle. It's just what you hustle. Trump had hustled land and buildings. I'd hustle jail cells. I told the warden to sign me up.

■   ■   ■

Things changed for me really fast. Every morning, I got up and went to my office, where there was a giant corkboard on the wall with all the prisoners' photos tacked up under their assigned cells. You could look at that thing and know exactly who was supposed to be where and with whom. Each day, someone was paroled or transferred 'cause of their job, or, if they wanted to go to school, they had to move to One Building, or if they hated their cellie and couldn't get along anymore, they'd ask for a change of scenery. I'd count up the vacant beds and cells that I had, call the intake building to see who was moving in, and figure out where to put them.

There was always a list for Four Building. Everyone wanted in. Four Building had single showers 'cause it used to be used as the SHU, and the showers were designed to hold one prisoner at a time. It was much safer than the other buildings, where they showered guys one hundred prisoners at a time. It was a big perk of living in Four, and I was even more spoiled 'cause once I was the slumlord, I could jump in the showers at 4:00 p.m. while all the other guys were heading back to their cells. I'd have them completely to myself, and still make it back to my cell in time for 4:30 count.

So every day, I had tons of requests to move to Four. I'd make the rounds of all the other buildings to speak with the slumlords to negotiate deals for certain moves, to scope out any problem people beforehand. Mostly, it was an excuse to stretch my legs, and have some freedom. I could have called them instead. I preferred the walk. I knew by showing my face around, I'd have more juice. I was free-range.

Suddenly, I was wheeling and dealing. I no longer needed money from outside people. To get a good cell from me, it would cost a guy around $20 to $50, to pay off his current building's slumlord, and then another $20 to $50 on my end. If he wanted a cell with two doors, or one of the cells at the end of a tier that had more peace and quiet, those cost more.

If he wanted a specific cellie, that would cost four or five packs of cigarettes. Some guys would just hand me two cartons of cigarettes and say, "Move me upstairs or move this person in." After that initial $50 down payment of sorts, they were good with me. Anything else they wanted was a favor. Now, if some guy showed up with just one or two lousy packs of cigarettes, I'd give him the eye. A pack or two wouldn't get you much help from me.

With that said, I was fair. I didn't charge somebody more 'cause I didn't like them, or 'cause of the color of their skin. I didn't charge them more if we were supposed to be enemies. Word spread quickly among the inmates that I didn't play favorites, and the job seemed to get a lot less risky. Guys weren't so pissed or jealous. Most of the guards appreciated that there was less violence among the prisoners, and a substantial reduction in the drugs that made it to the floors.

Every so often, I'd get a problem inmate who made my life a living hell. Rick James was one of those guys. He showed up in 1996. He was transferred from another prison and was a real pain in the ass. The lieutenant from Three Building walked over to my office and told me, "I need you to put Rick James into Four Building. He needs to be in a more protected, less violent area." I wasn't crazy about the idea of him coming. After my experience with Todd Bridges at County, I knew having a celeb on the tier was gonna cause problems. There was nothing I could do to stop it. They brought him over to the first floor, and I found him a cell. Guys immediately started paying him to sing songs.

Rick was a drug addict, and one by one, he lost cellie after cellie. Every time I put a guy in there, Rick would cause them to fuck up. Guys were trying to stay clean, but Rick just couldn't keep it together. I'd finally had enough of his bullshit. Rick and I got into an argument, cussing each other out. I didn't know Ray was standing behind me. Ray was a huge guy, very muscular. The next thing I knew, this fist flew over my head and knocked Rick James out.

I spun around. "What the fuck was that for?"

Ray just shrugged. "I got tired of him being a crying bitch. That is all that man ever did. Cry about everything." Ray spoke the truth, but it wasn't gonna save him.

I yelled at Ray, "You are going to the hole!"

Fortunately, Rick James didn't see who hit him. I don't know how he missed it. I don't look nothing like Ray, that's for sure. Ray's black. I'm white. Ray's huge, I'm small. It turned into a big investigation. The officers asked me what happened, and I said I didn't know. I played dumb. "I just turned around and there was a whole bunch of black people, which one was I supposed to pick out?" A corrections officer named Steve Larson, who was a lieutenant and my boss at that time, said, "Come on, Shorty, you know who did it." I told him, "I'm not telling you." He whispered, "I just wanna know, so I can shake the man's hand." Turns out, Rick James was driving the corrections officers crazy, too. They hated him.

For the next three years, I ruled Four Building as the slumlord. At the end of each day, I had to give a daily report to all the corrections officers about our numbers, our ethnicity balance, our gang affiliations, etc. There was paperwork for every minor detail. I didn't mind. It was a small price to pay for the perks. I had so much juice, so much authority, so much power, I got away with everything. I became almost untouchable. The guards couldn't mess with me, 'cause I knew all the lieutenants and the captains. If some guard was bothering me, I'd just ask my lieutenant to get them off my ass. Scott would tell them, "Don't fuck with the little guy." Sometimes, I even got the guards overruled, which was not always an intelligent thing to do. There were some guards who comingled with the inmates, and they would help set up other guys. You had to really watch yourself with those guys.

When Ray was paroled, I even went so far as to never give myself another cellie. I kept my cell a single. Every now and then, if it got overcrowded, I'd stick somebody in there, but the minute something came open, I scooted them out. I was not the easiest person to live with. Then or now. But nobody else got to live alone. I pushed the personal perks of the job as far as they would go, but I never allowed the job to be used for drug trafficking or for setting some guy up to get beat down. I learned how to play fair and sort of forced the guys in my building to do the same. Not everyone was happy with me about that, but I realized I couldn't keep everyone happy all the time. If most of the guys were happy, that was good enough for me.

I got pretty good at managing people and personalities. I got pretty good at negotiating terms, and talking shit out to find a mutually agreeable compromise. I learned to curb my temper and keep the peace, which took some doing. And more than anything, I figured out how to organize and manage a huge system, to keep it running smoothly, and to do it well enough that I didn't have to be watched with an eagle eye.

The more freedom I got, the more responsibility I took on, the happier I was. It's gotta sound weird to people from the outside, but for me, the slumlord job at Folsom was one of the best things to happen in my life. It forced me to grow up and "get a job" in that legit sense of handling a business. It prepped me to be in charge. It gave me the experience I'd need much later to run my own company.

I didn't know it then, but looking back now, it's pretty damn clear. Being the slumlord at Folsom was my unofficial MBA training program.

■　■　■

There's a myth that guys mark each day served on the walls of their cells, but that's not true at all. The only time you mark the days is when you're in the hole, and even in there, we were lucky enough to have books to read. About six months before my release, I started to feel a change in me. I did start to keep track of the days in my head, and it made me anxious all the time. Folsom was really getting to me. Things bothered me that had never bothered me before. Freedom was so close. I felt like I had to really be on high alert. Guys or guards that don't like you will plant drugs or needles in your cell, or on your person, just to screw you out of going home. I became more careful with my temper, and trust me, that was hard. I had to be cautious of who I hung around. I didn't trust many people. Instead of going out to the yard for rec time, I'd sit and play games. I did my best to keep out of trouble. I stayed inside more. When you went out to the yard, you had to stay out there for a set number of hours. You couldn't just go in and out as you pleased. If I did walk into the yard, and I could sense that something was wrong, I'd turn right around and go back inside. If I heard about things that might happen, or that something was gonna go down, I made sure I was not around. I'd get myself to another building. If I heard gunfire, I'd just stay put. I wasn't gonna risk ending up in a fight or in a situation that could keep me locked up. I even trained my friend Tony to take over the slumlord job. I relinquished my position, gave away any contraband I had stored in my lockers, and just bided the rest of my time. Better safe than sorry.

As the days got closer, my circle of people got smaller and smaller and smaller. Some guys backed off 'cause I was leaving and it was too hard for them to watch people go, and know they were never getting out. Some guys I had to let go. They were relationships that were just gonna get me into trouble. They weren't worth another day behind bars. I absolutely did not wanna go back to Los Angeles. I had friends in San Francisco. Tony's wife, Debbie, was gonna let me live in their guest room, and I even had a job lined up doing clerical work for a concrete recycling factory next to Candlestick Park. I petitioned to get my parole transferred, but just like I'd faced after DeWitt, I came up against the political bullshit that is the prison system. Two weeks before my release, the news came back that I couldn't parole in San Francisco. Never mind that I had no place to live in Los Angeles, and no job lined up down there. It was a slap in the face. I was trying to succeed. I was trying to set up a better situation, but they wanted to ship me right back to where I'd gotten into trouble in the first place. It made me mad, but then I just told myself that I do what I gotta do. Now where would I stay? How was I gonna make money? How would I stay away from the projects?

It looked like I was stuck with Heather. If there's one thing prison confirms, it's that you've made some pretty shitty decisions in life. But moving in with Heather . . . that might have topped the list for Single Stupidest Idea Ever. Heather was a Little Person who lived in Los Angeles. Her roommate was a Mexican woman whose boyfriend was one of the Northern Mexican gang guys I'd met at County. Once he found out his girl's new roommate was a Little Person, he assumed I'd like her, 'cause you know, all us Little People must get along or some such shit. In truth, I prefer my women tall. Really tall. Like six-feet-tall tall. But being that I still had a year left in Folsom, I figured I couldn't be picky. It wasn't like I had a lot of choices, unless I wanted to swing the other way, and I didn't, and good luck trying to hook up with a female prison guard. It's not like it's never happened in prison, but it was very rare. So I agreed to the setup.

I can just imagine that conversation. Heather's roommate saying to her, "Hey, my man's got this friend. He's, uh, you know . . . shorter . . . like you. And if you want, I can set up a blind date. But there's just one thing . . . he's in prison."

Now, any woman willing to date a guy behind bars has gotta have some problems. I guess the appeal comes from knowing exactly where your man is that night. (Unless, of course, your He is messing with a Him. Which happens.) Then there were the guys that had three or four girlfriends on the outside. I'd watch in awe as they juggled phone calls and visits and letters, and even with all the downtime in prison, I had no idea how they did it. There was this one guy, Scarborough, who was a major player until a guard walked in and told him, "You may wanna cancel your visitation today. Your wife is kicking your girlfriend's ass right now." Catfights in the visiting area were common. Scarborough just turned on his heel and said, "Tell my wife I'm in the SHU." The guard laughed. "Wife? I think you just became a divorcé!"

Heather's roommate had been coming back and forth from prison for years. She must have filled Heather's head with all kinds of stories, so I didn't expect nothing to come of it. Apparently, Heather was game. That should have been the first sign. We started talking over the phone. There were pay phones in the building, but I could call from my office anytime. I kept my calls to a minimum until we'd exchanged Polaroid pictures. Once I saw she wasn't horse-faced, we started writing more letters, and I called more often. Every call went collect and at $15 for like ten minutes, it was a total rip-off. We really ran up her bill, but she didn't seem to mind. Our conversations were always fine. Nothing too endearing. I wasn't looking to fall in love. In fact, not to seem cold, but to me, our "relationship" was a way to mark time. I certainly didn't need her for cash. I was making enough selling cells. But prison could be a really lonely place. To have a few phone calls. To write some letters. To have a few visits. To kiss a couple of times. It was a much needed distraction. It made the day move a bit faster. Gave you something to think about at night.

It was a whole process to come see me. First, Heather had to apply to get permission to visit. Then they had to run a background check on her. Then she had to get on an approval list for a specific date. Then she had to drive all the way from Los Angeles to Sacramento. Then, once she made it to Folsom, she had to sit for two hours while they put everyone through a security check. Visitors couldn't bring anything in with them at Folsom. Not books or photos to show. They had to buy the food that was sold there. If they wanted to give you money, they had to leave it on your books, deposit it into your account. They walked in with nothing and walked out with nothing.

And that was just what they put outsiders through. On my side of the bars, any guy seeing a visitor had to strip naked, bend, and cough. Before the visit and after the visit. It's not an exaggeration to say visitation was a literal pain in the ass. Not to mention I really didn't care for the whole routine 'cause I stood at the same level as everybody else's naked junk.

I was always willing to bend and cough to see Janet or Uncle D., but after three or four hours of talking with Heather, I'd get bored. It's not like we even had the option of conjugal visits, so kissing and talking were all we could do. Four hours of talking—enough! I'd just shoot a look at the guards, and one of them would walk over, tap his flashlight on the table like a warning, and tell me, "Time to go back to work, Shorty." I'd put on a real show of being disappointed. Then shoot the guard a nod of thanks. I always appreciated that they helped me out that way.

I never had any intention of staying with Heather after I was paroled. I wanted to start my life over, do my own thing, and leave the past behind me. Unfortunately, the CDC had other plans. They paroled me to Los Angeles, and I really didn't have any other option. I was unemployable, broke but free. I had to live somewhere, anywhere, away from trouble. Reluctantly, I agreed to move in with Heather. She was thrilled.

The last day I woke up in Folsom was a good, good day. I'd made it through the night without any problems. Usually the night before your release, the guys jump you in a pileup, and kind of pummel you, or they'll grab your neck and twist the skin to make it look like you have a hickey. Somehow, I'd managed to avoid both of those. I'd given away my TV, my radio, anything I had of value to friends who were staying behind. It would have been selfish to carry it out with me.

That morning, Officer Lawrence and Lieutenant Centurino came to walk me from my cell to R&R, reception and receiving. I hadn't been in R&R since the day I arrived. They shook my hand and said, "Good luck and don't fucking come back." Janet sent me some street clothes. I changed into those, then sat and waited and waited and waited for them to process me. This huge, Southern, corn-fed boy, a corrections officer, stuck his head out and yelled at me, "Hey, Shorty, you come back here and I'll beat the shit out of you." I flipped him off. "You ain't ever gonna see me again!"

I walked out of receiving and reception and saw those big old gates. My friend Tony's wife, Debbie, was waiting for me on the other side, sitting on the bumper of her purple truck. It was an amazing feeling. They may have brought me in by bus, but I walked out on my own two legs. It felt like a movie moment. I took that long walk to the gate, past the gun towers. I'll never forget hearing one of the officers call out to me, "Hey, Shorty, your bed will be waiting for you." But I knew I was never coming back. Ten years, ten months, and ten days had passed since my arrest. It was time to start a whole new life.

The Chipmunk

Debbie gave me a big hug and welcomed me back to the world. I climbed into the passenger side of her truck and looked back as we drove away. It wasn't a sense of relief I felt. I wouldn't call it that. I was prepared to leave. I'd had ten years of knowing the exact day I'd go home. But leaving Folsom, what I felt was . . . hungry. "Debbie! Take me to a good fucking Italian restaurant!" Debbie just laughed. We had a meal. A big, traditional, delicious Italian feast, then Debbie drove me over to see Ray's parents on Haight Street. Ray wasn't there. He was already back in jail. He wasn't robbing people anymore, but he just couldn't stay off drugs, a violation of his parole.

I purposely booked the last flight from San Francisco to Los Angeles. I wanted to spend as much time as I could as a free man, 'cause the next morning, I had to report to my parole officer and move in with Heather. When I landed in Burbank, she and her friend Lena were there to pick me up. I'd barely had a day to stretch my legs, and now I was moving in with a girlfriend I barely knew.

I made the conscious decision to stay away from the projects. I didn't want to go see my old homeboys or even Mama Myrt, Little Al, or Cerisse. In the years that I'd been locked up, we'd lost touch. Mama Myrt had her hands full with other family members in jail, namely, Little Al, who couldn't stay out of prison. Cerisse was popping out babies every year. She was on her sixth, and her family life was her priority now. And as for Coco, my first pit bull, he had died while I was in Folsom. There was no reason for me to go back to Nickerson, so I went on the lam from my friends and family.

Unbeknownst to Heather, I kept trying to get my parole transferred to San Francisco. She thought I was applying for jobs and going to interviews, but really I was dealing with the transfer paperwork and registering for general relief. I'd left prison with $200 in gate money. That's all I had to my name, so I applied for welfare and food stamps until I could either transfer to San Francisco and start my job, or find employment in Los Angeles. I had to have some way to eat. They approved me for $400 a month of relief and $100 of food stamps. How in the hell I was supposed to live on that, I didn't know. In all the time I'd lived in the projects, I'd never been on welfare. In prison, my top hourly pay rate was twenty cents an hour, but I'd never been strapped, 'cause I had a monopoly on cigarettes. Applying for welfare was humiliating. The lady who processed my form didn't even believe I'd actually been in prison. She kept fighting me about my application. She had her city job and she thought she was King Tut. I couldn't give up. I had no other choice. I had to deal with her.

The only good part about being in L.A. was going out dancing. I still loved to dance, so Heather, Lena, and I went out a lot, and everywhere we went, we were the center of attention. My dancing caught the eye of one of Lena's friends, Chris, a young woman who worked for Universal Studios. She approached me and said, "No pun intended, but we are short on Little People. I wanna give you a dancing job at Universal." I'd been out about a month, and the transfer to San Francisco was looking less likely by the day. I said, "I'm not taking off my clothes!" She laughed at me. "No, no. It's in the theme park. That's the catch." As long as I could keep my clothes on, I was game. "What do you mean, catch?" Chris kind of blushed with shame. "It's Alvin from Alvin and the Chipmunks." I didn't even have to think. "Hell no! I'm not into that fucking crap." But then she said, "It's good money." That stopped me in my tracks. I needed money desperately. "How much?" She had me now, and she knew it. "It's a hundred and fifty dollars a day. You can make over a grand a week." It was like . . . Houston, we have landed. I shook Chris's hand. "Where do I sign up?"

Chris sent me straight to Human Resources. She'd already seen me dancing, so I didn't have to audition again. I was terrified to fill out the paperwork. I knew if they found out about my criminal history, I wouldn't get the job. They were a huge corporation catering to families and kids. When it came to the question "Have you ever been convicted of a crime?" I checked the "No" box.

I wanted to work. I didn't wanna be on welfare for the rest of my life. I'd been sitting in front of Heather's computer every day, trying to track down paralegal work. I knew there was no chance in hell anyone would let an ex-con become a lawyer, but I thought maybe, just maybe they'd let me use my paralegal skills to get a foot in the door. I found out nice and quick that any work in law enforcement or the judicial system was a total pipe dream for me. Universal seemed like my only option. That night, at home, I waited by the phone, expecting a call telling me, "We're sorry, sir. You have a criminal record a mile high." That call never came. A week later, I was onstage shaking my furry ass in front of a thousand screaming kids, five shows a day, six days a week.

I loved it. I loved standing in front of a crowd and hearing all those kids laughing and clapping and singing along. I loved the lights and the crowds and the spectacle of the show. I loved hanging with the other performers, all of us a bunch of characters whether we were in or out of costume. I loved that nobody was trying to live a "regular" life. All these artists were their own bosses. They worked as extras on TV shows or stand-ins for the movies. Some were in commercials or touring the country with live shows. Everyone had a dream, and they were chasing it. They had great stories, and I admit, I got some stars in my eyes. It was strenuous work, but I loved it.

Heather did not. She didn't like that I was starting a new life. She didn't like that I was happier than I'd been in a long, long time. Jealousy reared its ugly head, and then jealousy turned to rage. The "Bride of Chucky" was now in residence, and she was showing her true colors. I didn't know it before, but I found out quickly that Heather was addicted to crystal meth. She'd blown through three inheritances like they were nothing. When I moved in with her, she had nothing, even though I knew she'd inherited seventy-five grand from one death, and another hundred grand from another family member's death. Where all that money had gone, I had no idea. She had nothing to show for it but a lot of emotional baggage. Her mom, her dad, and her sister had all passed away. The whole family was wiped out. I thought they were cursed. I didn't know that all her relatives were dying 'cause of drugs.

Maybe that's why Heather was on a mission to have a baby. It was her one and only goal, to start a family. She lied and told me she was on the pill, but when the pregnancy test came back positive, I knew I'd been played. I also knew I wasn't ready for a kid. I didn't panic, and it turned out I didn't need to. Her body, like most Little women, couldn't hold the pregnancy. She had a miscarriage. I hated that she had to suffer, but I'd be lying if I didn't say I was relieved.

After she lost the baby, Heather became suspicious of my every move, and started hounding me with questions, going through my things looking for proof of some imagined affair. She'd accuse me of "using her" for her money, of taking advantage of her, but she didn't have nothing to use! One night, we were watching TV, when out of the blue she said, "You know, if you ever cheat on me, I will run my head through the TV, then call your parole officer and tell him that you threw me into it." I kept my eyes on the screen and tried to remain very calm.

I managed a "Really?" She glared at me. "I'll make sure you violate your parole so you get sent back to jail. Then I'll know where you are and I can control you." Turns out, the Bride of Chucky had done this before. She wasn't just the roommate of a convict's girlfriend. She was also a convict's ex-girlfriend. In fact, she'd successfully controlled him for years, sending him back behind bars over and over again. The only reason she was fooling with me is that he was locked up and gone. And that idiot kept coming back to her.

After that threat, in the back of my head, I was screaming to myself, "Run, Shorty, run!" I saved up some money, and a few weeks later, when the Bride of Chucky left for work, I grabbed a friend to help me clear out. I made sure the apartment manager oversaw my move 'cause the crazy bitch had told me plainly that if I ever left her, she would take a sledgehammer to the walls and blame me for it. The apartment manager shook my hand and wished me luck. I was gonna need it.

■ ■ ■

Working as Alvin, I met several other Little People making their living onstage. There was one guy, Dave Myers, who'd known me since I was a kid. I'd met him back in third grade, when my parents had forced me to mingle with Little People. He was an okay guy, a friend of the family, and even though he knew all about my past criminal record, he started hooking me up with outside jobs. I could make a one-day appearance as Mini-Me or as a leprechaun and walk away with three hundred bucks. It was easy money, compared to the five or six shows a day I was doing at Universal. The Alvin show was hard work. I always played Alvin, and Alvin had the most dancing to do. Every once in a while, I'd have to stand in for Theodore, but the supervisors hated it 'cause I was an arrogant Theodore, and that character was supposed to be shy, calm, and quiet. Either way, I sweated my balls off in those costumes, under a hot blazing sun, covered from head to toe. What had seemed like a fortune, $150 a day to dance, in reality broke down to less than thirty bucks a show. Any extra I could make to supplement my income was welcomed.

After every show, we'd go out into the audience to shake hands, hug the kids, and take photos. We weren't allowed to speak to the kids, just make gestures and hop around. For the most part, I liked the audience participation, but every so often, you'd get a kid who would pop you in the head. It took everything I had inside me not to pop them right back! Backstage, Dave would tease me, "I wonder if Mommy knows her kids are hugging an ex-con." We'd crack up. Nobody but Dave knew. But he'd always been a great guy, so I trusted him, and when I escaped from the Bride of Chucky, he let me stay at his apartment for a few weeks until I could find a place to live.

I found an apartment in Long Beach, and my old cellie from Folsom, Ray, moved in with me. He was back out of prison again and needed a place to stay so he could get some distance between him and his old ways in San Francisco. Living together was just like old times. Only this time, we had our own rooms. We fell into our usual dynamic. Ignore each other if we weren't feeling social, hang out when we were. It was good to have Ray back in my life.

The gigs with Dave were few and far between, so I took a second job to try to get ahead. I applied to be a personal banker at Bank of America. I took the class they offered, and passed their test with a score of 100 percent. They hired me for their Glendale office, to work the night shift. I'd work at Universal all day, take the bus to my Bank of America job, get back on the bus, fall asleep until I'd reach my apartment in Long Beach, sleep for an hour or two, get back on the bus, and head to Universal. It was a vicious cycle.

That went on for four months, until one evening at Bank of America, my supervisor called me into his office. He put me on the phone with the corporate office. They said, "We just pulled up your criminal record. Is this you?" I must have muttered under my breath, "I'm through." My supervisor laid it out for me: "You've got a choice. You can resign, or we can terminate you." I chose to resign.

The next day, I called Janet and told her what happened. She must have told Linda, 'cause a few days later, Dad called to chew me out. He thought it was a travesty that I'd lost such an important job, asking, "What are you gonna do with your life?" I'd defend myself. "I'm dancing onstage! I'm enjoying myself. I don't have to report to fucking nobody." It was true. Despite the grueling schedule, the sweaty costumes, and the kicking kids, I enjoyed performing. My dad thought I needed to settle down. "But why? I missed ten years of my fucking life. Let me catch up!" He pushed. "You've gotta be like everyone else. With the home and a car and a wife and some kids." It made no sense to me. "Hello! Why? So I can be fucking miserable like you? No, thanks!"

I wasn't worried. I knew I'd find something else. The only place that would hire me was a phone sex operation. I processed the credit card information as the girls sat beside me, filing their nails and picking their teeth, yelling, "Yeah, daddy, do me, do me!" Learned my lesson with that job. Never call a phone sex line. There's nothing sexy about it.

I didn't have a car and I was getting about four hours of sleep a night. I'd head home on the Blue Line, fall asleep, make it all the way to Long Beach, and be halfway back to Los Angeles before I'd wake up. I was so used to the structured life in prison. In Folsom, I sat around and watched the same TV shows every single day. The same newscast in the morning. The same news in the afternoon. *Mr. Belvedere. Frasier. The Golden Girls.* My life outside was a complete disaster. I loved my job at Universal, but nothing was consistent. Did I wanna go back? Hell no. But the structure was comforting and in some weird way, I missed it. Real life was chaos.

It didn't help that the Bride of Chucky was stalking me. Eventually, I had to petition the court for a restraining order. She was infuriated that I had had the nerve to abandon her, and I wasn't sure what she would do. I made sure the restraining order had explicit language saying she wasn't allowed to be inside the Universal theme park. It didn't matter; she snuck in.

I was up onstage, shaking and shimmying and playing with the audience, when I felt a cold chill go up the white of my chipmunk stripe. There she was, glaring at me with those crazy eyes. The Bride of Chucky surrounded by sweet, innocent kids. I almost fell off the stage when I saw her. I felt my mouth go dry, and I panicked. Then I remembered, I had a few minutes backstage between scenes. As soon as the lights went down, I ran backstage and ripped off my Alvin head. I grabbed an assistant stage manager and terrified her with a frantic "Call security! Now!" There was no time to explain. My music cue came up and I had to run back out onstage. As I danced and tumbled, I caught a glimpse of Heather house right. She was closer and I swear to God, the veins in her neck were throbbing. Thank God, there was another short break between scenes, and I ran off as fast as I could. Once again, I ripped off the Alvin head. By this time, security had mobilized. I gave them the super-abbreviated version, which sounded wacked-out and breathless: "Restraining order. Crazy bitch. Audience. She might try to kill me!" To be honest, I was more afraid of the Bride of Chucky than I'd ever been of any Neo-Nazi. Neo-Nazis at least followed gang law. This bitch was off the reservation.

But it was my cue again, so I suited back up and ran out for the finale. Through the eye holes, I could see the security guards in the audience trying to find her. There were kids everywhere, and Heather was their same height. They couldn't really tell where she was, so I started dancing and trying to point at her with my tail, nod my chubby chipmunk cheeks in her direction. Finally, one of the guards caught on, and a swarm of seven security officers circled her. I just kept dancing my heart out as they lifted her up and carried her past the terrified parents pulling their kids closer. She was screaming like a banshee, "I AM NOT LEAVING HERE UNTIL I GET TO SEE HIM! I WILL CUT HIS FUCKING DICK OFFFFFFFFFFFFFF!!!!!!!"

■ ■ ■

I didn't need another girlfriend. What I needed was a car and a dog.

First things first. I bought a Mercury Capri convertible from my friend Kacic, then I bought a leash, a few cans of food, and a bowl for water. Ray and I drove over to Lacy Street and stepped into the North Central Animal Shelter. An old friend of mine, Garrence, was working there. The shelter was in desperate need of renovation, and the barking and smells were what I expected. What I wasn't prepared for was row after row of abandoned, brutalized, and scarred pit bulls. In the ten-plus years that had passed since I'd had to leave Coco with Little Al, pit bulls had been demonized. The Centers for Disease Control had published a study on dog bite–related fatalities, and determined that "pit bull terriers or mixes thereof" and Rottweilers accounted for a larger percentage of fatalities than any other breed. The result was pounds full of bully breeds.

But here's the thing, that report ultimately said that "generic non-breed-specific, dangerous dog laws can be enacted that place primary responsibility for a dog's behavior on the owner, regardless of the dog's breed. In particular, targeting chronically irresponsible dog owners may be effective."* In plain English, don't blame the breed, don't blame the dogs, blame the owners. But that didn't matter. Pit bulls were now the enemy. Their reputation got so bad, and their numbers were so overwhelming, that the San Francisco Society for the Prevention of Cruelty to Animals renamed them "St. Francis terriers" to try to help get them adopted.

The North Central Animal Shelter wasn't nearly as proactive. The place was the Folsom of pit bulls, filled with stocky, wounded warriors trapped behind gates. Their accommodations were not so different from the ones I'd left behind—concrete floors, flimsy bedding, a steel bowl, and food through a slot. I shuddered at the similarity. My God, there were so many. Dozens and dozens of pit bulls sleeping, staring, pacing, shaking. How in the hell could I possibly only choose one?

Garrence said, "Let me know if you want any of these." That's when I saw her. She was a thick girl with a short, silky coat and floppy, folded triangles for ears. She wore her brown fur like an open jacket, exposing a white chest and tummy. The white continued up the front of her neck and circled her mouth and nose, then met again in a thin line that traveled right up the middle of her square head. The effect was as if she'd glued two brown pork chops on either side of her face. She had high cheekbones, Nixon-like jowls, and soulful, searching eyes. It was love at first sight.

---

* "Breeds of dogs involved in fatal human attacks in the United States between 1979 and 1998," special report, The Centers for Disease Control, 1999.

I looked on her card and it said she was being euthanized. I said, "Garrence, what the hell!" He explained that she was on death row, scheduled to be euthanized that day. That did it. This brown-eyed girl was coming home with me. I said, "No, she's not. I want her." Garrence pulled her out of the cage and took her up front for processing. Only, the vet wouldn't let me take her home. He said she needed to be fixed, and that I could come back later in the evening to pick her up. Fine. I left. But later that night, when Ray drove me back to the shelter, the vet still wouldn't release her. They hadn't fixed her, and in fact, they were just getting ready to put her down. If I'd shown up ten or fifteen minutes later, she would have been dead.

All those anger management classes I'd taken back in the Youth Authority went flying out the damn window. I started screaming and cussing and yelling and demanding to see her. It wasn't an approach that worked well with a city employee. The vet wouldn't tell me why she was being put down, and he wouldn't give her to me. I yelled, "I already paid for her. I paid for her to be fixed!" He told me to pick out another dog and he'd apply the fee to it instead. I didn't want another damn dog. I wanted my girl. I yelled at him, "Well, keep her tonight and fix her in the morning and I'll come back." The guy just eyed me, saying, "I don't like your attitude." I'd had it by now. I screamed at him, "I don't like *your* fucking attitude!"

The vet walked away to go get a security guard. Things were getting pretty nasty. Garrence pulled me aside and said, "Shorty, there's a gate in the back. Just take the dog. You paid for her. I'll let her loose back there. Go on." Ray rushed out to get the car and I snuck into the yard, where I found my brown-eyed girl waiting. I checked over my shoulders to make sure nobody was looking before I pulled the leash out of my pocket. It's like the sweet girl read my mind. She bowed her head and let me wrap the leash around her neck, and then we made a run for it. She seemed to know exactly how to get us out of that hellhole. She pulled me toward the back gate, and we both ran as fast as our legs could carry us. With some pushing and some prying, *whooooosh*, she was out, then *whooooosh*, I was out, and we were free!

Ray was waiting in the alley with my old, red Mercury convertible already running. My brown-eyed girl hopped into the backseat and I rode shotgun. We tore out of there like bats out of hell, laughing our asses off and knowing we'd done the right thing. They could keep my ninety dollars for a spay job they never did. I had my girl. My panting, pretty, stolen Geisha. We were Bonnie and Clyde. I caught a glimpse of her in the rear-view mirror, and I swear to God, she smiled.

■ ■ ■

Adopting Geisha inspired me to volunteer with a group called L.A. City Camp, which took kids out of the projects for a day and brought them to Disneyland or Universal Studios. I didn't realize how little effort it took to have a big impact on kids. I was just doing it to have fun. I didn't realize that in the process of having fun, the kids were actually learning and seeing a new world. With kids that young, there was real potential for change, and I saw a change in me, too. I could relax and be myself around Geisha and the kids. I didn't have to worry about backstabbing. I didn't have to worry about kids trying to betray me. These kids were pure of heart.

L.A. City Camp was started by a white guy named Bruce McAllister, who'd been so moved by the Rodney King riots, he wanted to help. He was a behind-the-camera guy who actually walked into the projects to figure out how to be of service. Everyone thought he was insane, but the nonprofit grew and grew until it had a board of directors and tons of celebs involved. I enjoyed working with them, but then I went to a few of their fund-raisers, and it seemed to me like they were more worried with how everything looked than the kids they were supposed to help.

I decided to start my own nonprofit instead. I teamed up with two guys, Terrell and David, and we started the Watts Youth Foundation, which many years later morphed into Shorty's Charities. We did basically the same thing that L.A. City Camp did, but on a more one-to-one scale. I knew the parents personally. We'd take the kids to movie sets, Universal Studios, a tour of the Queen Mary, even to fly kites. Wherever we went, whatever we did, Geisha went with us. The kids got used to seeing her, being around her, and even taking care of her. They'd willingly pick up her poop. Well, maybe not so willingly, but they had to learn how to take care of her if they wanted her to be around. They'd bring bags of food for her. I could see that she made a real difference with them. They stopped being scared of pit bulls, and started seeing them in a new light.

Seeing Geisha with the kids set off the first spark of an idea. What if I could convince kids in the projects that pit bulls weren't dangerous and shouldn't be used for fighting? How could that change things? Could I change things? I started reading every book I could get my hands on to learn the history of pit bulls. There were lots of different versions about their past, but most seemed to agree that originally they were bulldogs used for boar hunting and bull baiting. The books showed paintings of the dogs, dating as back as far as the 1500s, and they looked a hell of a lot like pits to me. Three hundred years later, once bull baiting was outlawed in England, they started breeding the bulldogs with terriers to make them smaller and more agile so they could use them for ratting and fighting. They purposefully bred the dogs to be people-friendly, so when the handlers would jump into the ring to separate them, the handler would be safe. Dogs that showed aggression toward humans, even in the middle of a fight, were usually killed.

As for the American Pit Bull Terrier, it was a combination of English and Irish stock brought to the United States for use as cattle dogs, "catch dogs" for pigs, and for fighting. When the American Kennel Club was formed, they refused to recognize pit bulls because of their fighting history, so a man named Chauncy Bennet formed the United Kennel Club specifically for the purpose of registering the breed. They'd been in America for hundreds of years, and through generations of selective breeding, they'd gotten bigger, more muscular, and stronger. The terrier part of them was nearly gone, which is

I was a sharp dresser
early on.

And I knew the value of a
good hat.

With CoCo, my mom's dog, on the brown plaid couch where we'd watch
TV together. I loved CoCo a lot and later named my first pit bull, Coco,
after her.

My maternal
grandmother, Nonnie.

With my paternal grandmother, Elsie.

In the law library at DeWitt, around 1991.

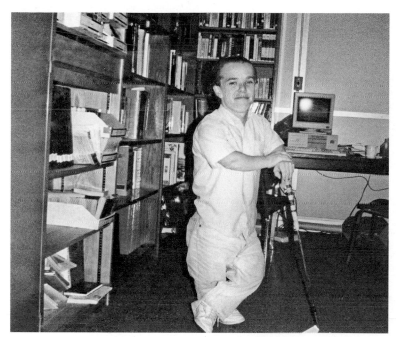

In my office at DeWitt.

Holding Zsa Zsa.

The Cat Man: feeding
time at DeWitt.

With Alvin and Jerry.

With Allison Queal.

On tour with the
Radio City Rockettes.

As Mini-Me.

With Loni Anderson.

From mini gladiator . . .

... to reality TV star. With Valentino, Hercules, and Bebi.

Bebi, Valentino, and Hercules.

Traveling with Hercules.

The whole family at home: Mussolini, Hercules, Domenico (top), Valentino, and Bebi.

why most people referred to them as pit bulls instead of by their full names.

I'd sit backstage between performances, dressed as Alvin, and read *Pit Bulls for Dummies* so intensely it looked like I was trying to memorize lines. One night Dave almost didn't wanna interrupt me, but he had a lead on a good job and he thought I'd be interested. A Little Person had dropped out of the Los Angeles cast of the Radio City Christmas Spectacular, and they needed someone to replace him fast. Was I interested? Hell, yeah, I was interested. Another job performing, instead of processing credit cards for the phone sex girls? "What do I need to do?" I quickly threw together an audition video, showing them my dance moves and telling them about my experience working as Alvin. I shipped it off to the New York casting office, and got the job.

Everybody knows that if you go to New York City between November and January, the Radio City Christmas Spectacular is running at Radio City Music Hall, but not everyone knows that they also have road companies that do a touring version in theaters all over the United States. Some of the companies "sit down" in a major city for a full holiday, like in Los Angeles or Miami, but other companies split their time between say, Branson, Missouri, and Cincinnati, Ohio.

All the shows, no matter where they were, ran for ninety minutes and followed the same script. They started with the Rockettes performing "Ring Out Those Bells," which would cause Santa to show up at the theater. There'd be more Rockette dancing, then a scene from *The Nutcracker* where a little girl would dream about opening her presents on Christmas Day, and dance with toy bears played by Little People in costumes. There'd be a bunch more singing and dancing with wooden soldiers, and then the show moved to Santa's workshop, where Little People played his elves.

The Los Angeles show ran at the Universal Amphitheatre, which is now the Gibson Amphitheatre, so I could actually keep doing my Alvin gig, and take on the extra Radio City show without having to give up either. I'd finish a Chipmunks show in the theme park, strip out of costume and run to the amphitheater, do a Christmas show, and then run back to the theme park and jump onstage as Alvin again. I'd run back and forth all day long. The only way I was able to handle both shows was because out of all the scenes featuring Little People in the Christmas Spectacular, I was only needed for one. All the other Little People were dancing in the Nutcracker scene, as baby bears, as moving snowmen, and as elves in Santa's workshop. Me? I only had to work for five minutes, as an elf in Santa's workshop. The guy I'd replaced had serious mobility issues and they'd only been able to use him as an elf. All the other Little People were pretty pissed off with me that I collected a full paycheck for five minutes of work. I didn't do shit and I got paid great, $1200 a week, on top of my Alvin salary. Like I'd hoped, I was able to quit processing credit cards for the phone sex company and joined AGVA, the union for dancers and theme park performers. I was a full-time performer now. I'd found my calling.

That's when I met Allison. Allison Queal had been doing

the Radio City show for years and she didn't like that I'd just waltzed in and landed the primo gig. She hated even more that I had the nerve to sleep in the dressing room while she was out there dancing her Little legs off. During the run, we couldn't stand each other. It was a mutual hate/hate relationship.

But Allison noticed something else I was doing besides sleeping between gigs. Whenever I heard about a gig that needed a Little Person, I'd hook up one of my fellow cast members with the job. I had my hands full with the Alvin and Radio City gigs. I couldn't take on any more work. So I'd turn down the jobs, but promise to help them find someone. I'd step into the dressing rooms and hook people up. It was a pretty easy way to turn all that animosity into goodwill.

After the Radio City show closed for the season, I got the idea that maybe I should open a talent management company for Little People. I was always trying to find an angle, always trying to find my next gig, and I thought, "Look at my Little People. They can be my crack. I can sell them, loan them out. I can be the pimp of Little People." I'd watched Uncle D. run his business for a year. It was the same principle as selling drugs. Little People were the product. I just needed to find a way to market them.

There weren't that many agents or companies willing to represent Little People. Most of us were repped by the Coralie Jr. Theatrical Agency, the first agent to take on Little People as clients. Coralie had been around since the '50s, and in all those years, she had somehow managed to keep her last name a secret. She refused to use computers; she kept all her business information in her head. She repped one-of-a-kind performers no one else would touch. She still had vaude-villians on her roster, over a hundred celebrity look-alikes, circus acts, animals, magic shows, snake charmers, armpit players, fire-eaters, you name it.

That was the problem. Everyone was with Coralie, and she played favorites. She only sent out the people who kissed her ass. The rest of us sat on ours. I finally got the nerve to leave her and move to Central Artists, but I found I was getting more and more direct calls from bookers needing talent. It just made sense to stop passing the information on, and instead start booking the jobs myself, managing the talent and taking a fee for my services. Word spread quickly among the Little People community that I was considering opening a legitimate business. Allison called from out of the blue. She said, "I want in."

Even though we butted heads at the beginning, I could tell Allison was on point. She'd show pictures of herself dressed up for all kinds of costume gigs and I realized she owned those costumes, and that's why she worked so much. Light bulb. Owning costumes led to work. She was the hardest worker I'd ever seen. She was always on the phone, hustling. She worked twelve hours a day. She was driven to work and I could never find people who impressed me in that way, who could live up to my standards. People weren't perfect, but I always expected them to be. Being a lady and a Little Person in the entertainment business, that was hard for Allison. She had earned my respect.

We may have hated each other in December, but by February of 2000, we launched Short Entertainment with a cheesy two-page website, business cards, a cell phone, and a fax machine. Allison handled the costumes and talent, and I handled the client relations. We mailed flyers announcing our new venture, and waited for the cell phone to ring.

Somehow, it worked. Turns out, clients liked our hands-on approach to booking. Instead of just shipping ten or twelve actors to their events, where they would have to deal with them individually, Allison and I would oversee each event, providing all the costumes, and handling the talent so our clients didn't have to lift a finger. Except to sign the check. Actors can be a real pain in the ass, and I can say that 'cause I've been one. So clients liked that I was in charge. The only person a client had to deal with was me.

Over the course of our jobs, we invested $20,000 in costumes, which turned out to be the smartest thing we did, and we housed all the props and outfits in Allison's house. We had over four hundred costumes. Elves, Oompa Loompas, leprechauns, drag queens, clowns, waiters, bartenders, Marilyn Monroe, Cher, Tattoo, Mini-Me, Elvis, and Frankenstein. All of them had to be specially made to fit Little People. If we didn't have it, and a client ordered a specialty character, I'd include the cost of the costume in my fee, and keep the outfit once the gig was over. Upkeep of the costumes alone was a full-time job. Allison had her hands full picking up and delivering and altering costumes for every gig.

I ran a tight ship with lots of rules. Why? 'Cause Little

People can be Little fuckers. I made my talent sign a ten-page morality contract before they came to work for me. I couldn't have kids visiting Santa catch one of his elves smoking. No mommy wants to explain that to her kid. I caught a bunch of Oompa Loompas at the Playboy Mansion sticking their cameras between girls' legs and under their skirts. At a charity event for cancer research in Vegas, the client had requested a tribe of pygmies, which was a fucking riot to see, and one of my Little fucks had the nerve to light up. At a CANCER benefit. I fired her on the spot and sent her home, dressed as a pygmy. It got to the point where Allison had to remove all the pockets from our costumes so there would be nowhere to stash shit—no keys, no nothing. Thus began the era of Shorty the Asshole Boss. I got a reputation among Little People as being mouthy and demanding, but Disney does the same damn thing to protect its brand, and nobody blinks an eye. With me, these Little bastards acted like I was oppressing them, like they were doing me a favor by existing. They didn't like it or like me very much, but the actors were making good money, so they kept coming back for more. And believe me, none of them turned down the work.

I'd spent nearly two years performing as Alvin, and I was ready for a change, so the following Christmas, instead of signing up for the Los Angeles Radio City show, Allison told me I should ask to go on tour instead. Technically, I wasn't supposed to leave the state of California. I was still on parole, and considered a violent offender, which meant I had to parole for the maximum number of years: three. The first parole officer they assigned me was an ass. He had the typical attitude. "You won't be out for long." I didn't even bother to learn his name.

Over the course of my parole, they switched me to five different officers. As long as I reported on my assigned day, wasn't arrested again, and came up clean on drug tests, I was considered a model citizen. I had only one more year left to report. I figured I could fly back and forth a few times and they'd never be the wiser for it, so I took a leave of absence from Universal Studios and headed to Branson, Missouri, with the Rockettes. If I'd known they were gonna send me to Branson, I'd have stayed in L.A.! There was a whole lot of nothing to do in Branson. The highlight of a Saturday night was a trip to the Walmart.

We were dark on Mondays, and flying out of Branson wasn't happening, flying out of Springfield wasn't happening, so once a month, I had to rent a car and drive all the way to St. Louis or Kansas City without letting anyone in the Radio City production office know I was gone. They had no idea I was an ex-con, so I couldn't tell them I had to report for parole.

I'd fly out Sunday night, turn around and report to my parole officer on Monday morning, then fly out Monday night or Tuesday morning and arrive in time for the Tuesday night call time. This worked pretty well for October and November, but once the weather started to get bad in December, it was a crapshoot. I got stuck in a snowstorm in December and missed a show. They put in my understudy, and when I was confronted about the no-show, I just claimed I'd had a death in the family.

I wasn't crazy about lying to people all the time, but there was no way to work unless I did. I figured I wasn't hurting anyone. I wasn't running drugs and I wasn't messing with the wrong crowd anymore. I was paying my bills, paying my taxes, and making ends meet as a performer. I'd never slip back into street life, of that much I was determined. I didn't even have the desire. Yeah, there were days when I'd think about how hard it is to make a buck in the real world, and compare it to how easy it was to make thousands and thousands of dollars dealing drugs or helping somebody out with their dirt. Then I'd think about all those months of jury trials. Of getting up every morning at 4:30 a.m., the bus ride, and being behind prison bars, and it was very clear. I'd rather be busting my ass to pay my bills than be stuck like that again.

It didn't mean I didn't fuck up every now and again. I ended up getting suspended for ten days from the Alvin show for knocking the tall actor who played the character "Dave" off the stage. This actor was notorious for stepping on us Little People and grabbing us roughly. He just wouldn't pay attention to where we were or how he handled us. After he stepped on me for the umpteenth time, I got mad and pushed him off stage. I knew I was in trouble when I saw my supervisor standing in the wings. He'd seen it all.

I got called into my boss's office. I felt like I was back in detention. My boss reprimanded me, "You've gotta write a letter of apology, Shorty." I protested, saying, "We've been bitching about this asshole for months and you guys haven't done nothing about him." My boss agreed with me, but said, "That doesn't mean you can violently push him off stage in front of an audience." I threw my hands in the air. "Violently? He may have landed violently, but I just bumped him." There was no compromise to be had. My boss drew the line in the sand. "You either apologize like I asked, or I will suspend you." I opted for the suspension.

I took it as a sign that it was time to move on. I started auditioning for TV shows and movies. At first, I was frustrated 'cause every time I went to an audition for a male Little Person, they didn't care about acting skills or talent. They wanted a certain look. An impish, elfish, deformed look, and I wasn't that. There were times when I'd come close. I'd get a callback for a speaking role, and some jealous Little Person would sabotage me by telling the casting director or producer that I'd been in prison. Every Little Person knew I'd been in the joint. They'd read about it in the Little People of America newsletter back in 1988 when I was arrested. Damn gossips, all of them! Most of the casting directors didn't care, but some producers were worried about putting an ex-con into a children's holiday movie. I lost a few jobs 'cause of those jealous fucks.

Eventually, I landed my first walk-on as an elf for *Ally McBeal*, and word got around that I was a hard worker. Then the credits kept coming. I did commercials for Miller Light, UPS, and Kia. For Miller Light, I played a gladiator. For UPS, I was an elf delivery guy, and for Kia, I was a leprechaun. I got to work with Verne Troyer on *Shasta McNasty*, and performed my first stunt as a wrestler for the pilot of *Los Luchadores*. I hadn't realized there was so much stunt work available for Little People.

In most movies, producers hire a Little Person to stand in or stunt double for the kid stars. Basically, the Screen Actors Guild says that everything has to be ready to go before a director calls the stars to the set for their scenes. The camera has to be positioned and the lighting has to be right, so every major star has a stand-in that looks like him. Jim Carrey's guy looks nothing like him, but he's the right height and hair color, which is all that's important. Eddie Murphy's guy, Bruce, is a dead ringer for Eddie. So much so that if there's a scene they can shoot from a distance, or looking over his back, they'll put Bruce in the shot instead. That's the way the business works when you're getting paid $25 million a movie. Some actors have their own photo doubles and stunt doubles, in addition to a stand-in. After working on a few sets, I couldn't watch a movie without trying to see who was doing what in each scene. Is it really Eddie or is it Bruce?

So many Little People hated stand-in work, they demanded higher pay than the regular union rate. Producers would get so fed up, they'd hire a tall person and put them on their knees. It was cheaper. Me, I'd work for scale just to be on the set, and I never complained. I wanted to learn as much as I could about stunts and movie production and how the whole process worked. I even went back to Universal and worked for their Wild West Show so I could learn how to jump off a three-story building.

The stunt guys would teach me how to fall and jump on their own time. They started me off by standing on a brick. A brick. I looked at them and said, "Can we start with something taller than me?" From there, they pushed me to go higher and higher, until I was ready to jump off a three-story building. The first landing was a rough one. I was supposed to land flat on my back but I didn't make it. I hit the fall pads in a sitting position and felt lightning rush up my spine, all the way through the top of my head. I couldn't move, think, or talk. I just lay there, tingling all over, and hoping I hadn't broken my tailbone. Then I thought maybe I was paralyzed. I tried wiggling fingers and toes, and those seemed to work. Within a few minutes, I could move again. I rolled off the hay-covered fall pad and headed back up, three stories into the sky. I couldn't let a bad landing end my stunt career on the first jump. I had to shake it off. I had to do that jump three or four times a night. Second show, I went running as fast as I could and just promised myself I wouldn't look down. You better believe I learned how to get myself flat before I hit the mats again. No more lightning up my spine. After that, jumping was nothing. It was second nature. I never thought about my physical safety. I didn't have a fear of heights. I knew what I was capable of doing, and I did it. If it seemed like I wasn't capable of doing it, then damn it, I'd figure out a way to do it.

Standing in and stunt doubling for kids opened even more doors, and suddenly, I was working with A-list stars like Bruce Willis on *The Kid*, or on *Tiptoes* with Matthew McConaughey and Gary Oldman; *Daddy Day Care* with Eddie Murphy and Jeff

Garlin; *Showtime* with Robert De Niro and Eddie Murphy; *How The Grinch Stole Christmas* with Jim Carrey; and *Call Me Claus* with Whoopi Goldberg.

Working on *The Grinch* was an eye-opening experience. Being on a multimillion-dollar set with Ron Howard and Jim Carrey felt like taking a college class on the Big Time. Those guys were real power players, but they treated everyone with respect, from the costumers to the stand-ins to their costars. I'd never worked in front of a green screen before, and they stuck me on top of a huge sleigh, dressed as an elf. Then they told me that Taylor Momsen's stunt double wasn't in that day. Taylor was the girl playing Cindy Lou Who. So it would be my job to dress up like Cindy Lou Who, and hang off the sleigh while it was shaking and rocking and flailing around in front of the green screen. That sleigh was fucking huge, but I held on. I was scared for my life. I was convinced I was gonna fall and break my neck, but we made it through the shot and I got some screen time—even if you can't tell it's me.

For *Daddy Day Care*, all the other Little People they'd hired to work were so busy eating at craft services, checking their phone messages, and complaining about the overtime hours that I ended up being used as the stand-in and the stunt double for most of the kids. I wasn't gonna complain about overtime. Between meal penalties and hours, I'd walk away from a day on the set being paid $300 to learn! I loved being on set. I wanted to understand how everything worked and what everyone did and who was who and how it ran. When the camera guy wasn't busy, I'd ask him questions. If the lighting guy had a minute, I'd talk to him. The whole crew took me under their wing and started giving me behind-the-scenes looks at their jobs. So when the cameras were rolling, and they quickly needed a stand-in for a kid, there I was, right on set and ready to go. I even stood in for the black kid 'cause they couldn't find the black Little Person when they needed him. They just stuck a black beanie on my head to account for his hair color. It paid off. On-screen, that's me on the riding lawn mower.

The producer Dan Kolsrud noticed I was a hard worker and eager to learn, so he called me over. He offered me the seat next to him. "Hang out here, Shorty. You'll have a front-row look." It was the equivalent of going to film school. Dan would explain to me all the politics and maneuvering that happened, and basically trained me as an apprentice producer for the remainder of my time on set. I ate it up. Producing was much more interesting to me than acting. It fed into my need to be in charge. To be an executive. To be the boss. The best part was, it was still related to the entertainment business, which I'd grown to love. I'd never had any intention of playing a bunch of stereotypical elves or Oompa Loompas or chipmunks. I'd never seen myself as that kind of guy. Yet, somehow, I'd fallen in love with Hollywood, with performing and entertaining people. Maybe producing was a way to be involved with the business and still be a businessman. Getting to know Dan better allowed me to see an entirely new side of the industry, and I was honored when at the end of the shoot, his production team sent me a crew jacket, unheard of for a lowly stand-in.

■ ■ ■

Work in the movies may have been educational and fun, but it wasn't steady, so when the offer to tour again with the Radio City Christmas Spectacular came up, I gave notice on my apartment in Long Beach, put all my stuff into storage containers, and loaded up the car for my trip to Cincinnati and Indianapolis, where the tour was "sitting down" in split cities. Four months of steady work was a good thing, even if it meant I had to dress up like a tutu-wearing bear and dance around.

Ray didn't wanna go back to San Francisco. He knew if he headed home, he'd use again and end up back in jail. He'd done pretty well staying clean since we'd been living together. We both drank and smoked cigars, but Ray'd been able to stay off the pipe, so I got him a job as a stagehand's assistant.

You should have seen us trying to pack my Mercury Capri convertible. There was me and Ray and all our suitcases and crap we'd need to live for the rest of the year. On top of that, we had Geisha and two adopted cats, Shitty and Hood Rat. Shitty was a terrible farter. On the days it rained, and we had to keep the windows up, she nearly killed us. We were quite a band of travelers. Two ex-cons, two shelter cats, and a pit bull in a Mercury Capri.

We didn't have to start rehearsals for three or four weeks, so we stopped by Vegas to hang with Tony's wife, Debbie, the lovely lady who'd picked me up from prison and fed me my first real Italian meal in ten years. She was still married to Tony, but Tony was a lifer. He wasn't getting out anytime soon, if at all, so Debbie moved to Las Vegas and took a job as a nurse at one of the local hospitals. Tony was petitioning the courts to be moved out of state, to be closer to her. They hoped her move would help his case. Every prisoner knew that if you could get out of the California system, you had a better shot at early parole, but so far, no luck. Tony was still back at Folsom in Five Building. Debbie was moving on with her life in Vegas. She loved the heat.

We spent a week with Debbie, then drove to Kansas City to stay with my sister Linda. I hadn't seen Linda for years, and we weren't much in touch, but it seemed stupid to be driving through her city and not stop to say hello. Plus, it was a free place to crash for a few nights. It didn't take long to remember why we hadn't been in touch. Linda was the family gossip. Anything I said to her would be repeated to Mom and Dad within a few hours or days. The three of them would gang up on me about improving my life, getting a real job, and settling down. They sat in judgment of me, and I didn't need the lecture. I told them all, straight out, "If I get a wife, I can't travel no more! I can't get a last-minute call and have to turn around and cancel a family vacation 'cause I got a gig. Or face those constant 'When you coming home?' questions. Trust me, I've been in relationships like that. I'm better off alone!"

It was true then and it's still true now. No woman wants to deal with a guy that's never home, flying all over the country. Even if I am home, I'm home with anywhere from three to six pit bulls in the house, on the couch, sleeping in my bed at night. Most women aren't happy about a house full of dogs, but there's no way I'm putting them outside. Any woman who tells me to put my dogs outside would find herself sleeping on my porch. My pits are my family. Love me, love my pits.

Linda wouldn't let Geisha into her house, and she was terrified 'cause she was a pit bull. Mom and Dad now had another reason to berate me: "You're gonna be killed by that dog!" I was glad to get out of there, and after that visit, I didn't speak to Linda again.

Once we got settled in Indianapolis, I sent a long e-mail to all of my family, excluding Janet, letting them know I'd had enough. I was tired of the shit. Linda was always starting fights. Creating drama. This kind of petty arguing had been going on since I was a kid, all the back talk, and nobody was ever happy with me. I let Linda have it. "I'm tired of the lectures about my career. The dog isn't gonna kill me. We fucking visit with each other, and everything is peachy keen, and then the minute I leave, you turn around and talk shit about me."

As for my parents, I couldn't have a phone conversation with Mom without Dad listening in on the other line. Mom couldn't even write an e-mail to me without Dad reviewing it first. It was a constant battle to have a relationship with my own mother. I was through playing their games.

The only family spared my rampage was Janet. To this day, my sister Janet has never asked me any questions about what happened on that night I was arrested. She may have sat through the trial, but she never needed me to tell my version of the story to her. Once I tried to, and she said, "It's done and it's over with and you're not doing those things today. You're my baby brother and you can't ever do anything wrong in my eyes." No matter what path of wrong I took, Janet was always there for me. I was grateful to call her my sister. I still am.

■ ■ ■

I was assigned to share a two-bedroom apartment with a Little Person named Ronald Lee Clark. Ronald was originally from South Korea, but his mom had left him at a police station when he was two years old. He was adopted, through the Little People of America organization, and ended up being raised by an American family in a small town called Choctaw, outside Oklahoma City. He seemed like a bit of a diva to me. He'd been a cheerleader for Christ's sake. Ronald wasn't thrilled to find out he was rooming with Geisha, Shitty the farting cat, Hood Rat, and two ex-cons. He didn't have much of a choice.

Ronald and I lived completely different lifestyles, but for the tour, we had to find a way to get along. We were sharing a rental car. I am the kind of guy who likes to be in my dressing room way before I need to be. Ronald was the kind of guy who didn't mind getting there five minutes after his call. He was always late. He liked to play things by ear. He'd hem and haw about decisions, and say, "When I wake up, we'll figure out a way to share the car." That wasn't cool with me. I wanted a schedule. If we had to be at work at two, then I wanted the car for two hours and he could have it for two hours before we needed to be at the theater. There were a few times when he had to get a cab to work 'cause he wouldn't move his ass fast enough for me.

There was another Little Person on tour with us named Sebastian Saraceno. Sebastian and I got along a lot better. Sebastian is an American of Sicilian descent, so we had our Italian heritage in common. He'd been working entertainment in Florida for a bunch of years, doing live performances with various radio stations and the Salerno Theatre. Seb was the kind of guy who couldn't nibble grapes in a grocery store, he was so by the book, so honest. That was his character. He was anal-retentive to the point of being annoying. Organized to the cue. I could tell that about him immediately. He was decisive. I respected that, and it helped that he was on tour with his girlfriend. They were living together, so he wasn't up in my grill all day long like Ronald. Seb didn't get on my nerves.

Eventually, we all became friends. Even Ray got along well with them. The whole gang of us would go out together and hang out. We ended up doing three more tours together. There are three pictures in three different shows of Seb and Ron holding me up, drunk. I introduced both the guys to Allison, and we added them to our roster of talent for Short Entertainment. We became tight.

Our apartment was on the creepy side of town. It was unsafe for the Rockettes to be living there, so eventually they moved the entire cast and crew to the Marriot Residence Inn. I was allowed to have Geisha—the hotel knew about her—but we had to keep the cats a secret. Then Ray decided he wanted to adopt a Boston terrier. We found a mom-and-pop pet store, and showed up with Geisha on a leash. Ray was looking over the Boston terriers when the woman who ran the place came over to admire Geisha and give her a rub between the ears. "Such a beautiful pit bull. As a matter of fact, we've got a box of pit puppies in the back. Their mother was hit by a car."

She took us behind the counter into the storage area, where a cardboard box of what seemed to be wiggling worms turned out to be six motherless pit puppies. As I leaned down to take a closer look, one cute guy stuck his head over the side of the box. He was mostly white, with a patch of black on his right hip and right shoulder, and a nearly perfect black circle around his right eye. I wasn't even looking for another dog, but I knew right then and there, he was mine. I bent down and whispered in his floppy ear, "I'm getting you." So much for the Boston terriers. We had our Mussolini.

■   ■   ■

As the Radio City tour was wrapping up its final performances, I had no plans for what to do next. I got it into my hard head that I needed to conquer New York City. I was off parole and free to move, and I thought I could expand Short Entertainment to include the Little People of New York. I mistakenly assumed there would be industry jobs and auditions available. Nobody else was repping Little People in the city. I thought I'd carve a niche for myself. Plus, I'd given up my apartment in Long Beach, so there was no "home" to go home to in Los Angeles anyway. Why not give New York a try?

The rents in Manhattan were outrageous, and forget trying to find a place for two pit bulls, two cats, and two ex-cons. I was about to give up on my plans, when I sat down backstage after one of the Radio City shows with Candace, the mom of one of the kid stars in the show. Candace and I had become friends during the run, and we often met after the bow to share a cigarette or a cigar, or go grab a drink. Candace heard the disappointment in my voice. She said, "Why don't you look in Pennsylvania? We're in Wilkes-Barre, and it's just ninety minutes from the city." She assured me that she made the drive back and forth all the time for her son's auditions. Candace sweetened the deal by promising me a job as an emcee for her dance competitions. She owned a whole slew of dance studios across the Northeast, called the David Blake Studios. She was a busy lady who promised she could keep me busy, too.

Now, any driver in Los Angeles will tell you they've spent ninety minutes in traffic just to get to the grocery store. Ninety minutes behind the wheel was not a daunting prospect to me 'cause I didn't really understand that driving from Wilkes-Barre to Manhattan actually took two to three hours. On a good day. Ignorance kept me blind, and I started searching for apartments through online newspapers and found a three-bedroom house in Glen Lyon for $460 a month. Glen Lyon looked like it sat right outside Wilkes-Barre, so I figured it was essentially the same kind of neighborhood. I was wrong. Glen Lyon was an old coal-mining town that was stuck in 1942. All the businesses had closed in the '70s and rows and rows of houses stood empty. All the young people had moved away, and everyone left was old and had known each other for generations.

When the tour was over, Ray and I said good-bye to Ronald

and Seb, packed up the Capri, and moved to Glen Lyon. Our arrival was greeted as though aliens had landed in a spaceship. People stared out their windows at us. A white midget and a black guy would have been bad enough. We had Noah's Ark in our car, and we'd even added to the family, adopting a gray, black-and-white pit bull puppy from a woman in upstate New York who'd rescued a litter that'd been abandoned by their mother. We named her Bebi, and moved her into the house with the rest of the zoo.

Nobody would talk to us, and Ray seemed to be the only black man within a fifty-mile radius. There were no auditions for Little People in New York, so there was no need for Short Entertainment to open an East Coast office. Allison was still in Los Angeles, running our business, but she'd always been better with handling talent, while I was the one who stirred up jobs. Now the only work I could scrounge together was emceeing for Candace, which I had to supplement with California unemployment checks. We'd made a big mistake moving.

That fact was confirmed when cops showed up on our front porch. I was in our basement and Ray was on the second floor of the house when Geisha and Mussolini started barking their heads off at the front door. Something was really wrong. I heard Ray clomping down the stairs, so I ran upstairs. The dogs just wouldn't stop, no matter how much we yelled. Something was really, really wrong.

When I made it to the living room, there were three cops on the porch. One had his foot against the front door and his gun drawn. I froze in place, and Ray did, too. No sudden movements. We were used to the LAPD. I yelled over the barking dogs, "What's going on here?" The police yelled back, "Did you call 911?" Ray and I just looked at each other. Neither one of us had called. "Is your phone off the hook? A phone off the hook will trigger an automatic call to 911 after a period of time." Sure enough, one of the dogs had knocked a phone off the hook. Ray righted the phone, but the police weren't going away. "Can we talk with you for a moment?"

Ray put the dogs away as the Pennsylvania good old boys made themselves at home in our living room. "Where y'all from?" I told them L.A., hoping they'd soon leave, but knowing we were in for a long night. The main guy loomed over me. "What the hell are you doing here?" I explained to him that I ran a talent management company. "Out of Pennsylvania?" he said. I clarified: "We work with a dance company in Wilkes-Barre. The David Blake School of Dance."

Apparently, I'd said the magic words. Suddenly, all the cops relaxed, and everyone got friendly. "You work for Mark and Candace and them? Well, that's a relief! Everyone in your neighborhood thinks you are drug dealers!" All the cops had a good laugh. "You gotta realize, we don't get that many midgets and colored guys around here." I thought Ray might explode, but I shot him a look like "get over it." Technically, Ray was a fugitive. He was still on parole, but never reported. No need to make trouble when we'd just gotten ourselves out of a mess.

Once word got out who we were, our neighbors transformed from enemies to friends. Our next-door neighbors were the Kielbasa Kings of Glen Lyon. They invited us over for dinner, for fresh kielbasa. We were an overnight sensation. It made life a bit easier, but I was still miserable in Pennsylvania. Then Jerry was killed.

Jerry was supposed to be moving out to join us when I got a call from an old friend, Darrell. Jerry had been in and out of prison for drugs, selling not using. He finally had stopped doing that shit, and had been out so long in this stretch that he was no longer on parole. But Jerry still loved to play dice, craps. He was always going back to the projects to play. He just couldn't break completely away from that neighborhood. The projects were still home to him, even though he didn't technically live there. He had to be around that world to feel comfortable. He was "institutionalized," as I call it. It cost him his life.

They were rolling in front of the gym. There was in-house beef going on with a gang. That gang came over and just started shooting anyone who was standing in front of the gym. Five people were shot. Jerry was shot in the head. He had nothing to do with what was going on.

Before that phone call, I'd always been an on-again, off-again recreational pot smoker. When I lived in Long Beach, I'd been more than that. I was smoking so heavily, it was slowing me down. Allison pointed out to me that the pot was making me lazy. It was affecting my daily life, but it calmed me way down, so I kept it around.

When Jerry died, I couldn't smoke anymore. I'd smoke and think about him getting shot. I'd smoke and think, "If Jerry had just moved out here with us, he'd still be alive." It made me so sad. I smoked my last stick of weed in Pennsylvania, then called up Debbie in Vegas and told her, "I've gotta get out of this hellhole." She convinced me to move to Las Vegas.

■ ■ ■

A few months before we were supposed to move, Geisha went into heat. None of my dogs were neutered or spayed. It wasn't something I considered important to do at the time, so Ray and I undertook the futile attempt to keep Mussolini away from my girl. We had no plan about timing their feedings or their pee breaks so they wouldn't run into each other. The right hand didn't know what the left hand was doing. It was inevitable. Mussolini would be a dad.

I may have read a lot about the history of pit bulls, but I knew nothing about breeding or responsible dog ownership. When Mussolini hopped on top of Geisha, he got stuck, and couldn't get loose. I was about to have a heart attack. I thought something was wrong with my dogs. I called Diana at the local pet parlor, freaking out. "They're stuck!" She had to calm me down. "That's what happens. Don't worry. They'll naturally release each other." Diana was right, but I knew we were still in trouble. Geisha was pregnant, and we'd have a litter of puppies to care for when we were supposed to be driving across country to our new life in Vegas.

Two weeks later, Bebi went into heat. This time, we locked Mussolini in a bedroom on the second floor, convinced we could keep him from becoming a dad for the second time. We were so stupid to think something like a door could hold Mussolini back. I was in the basement and Ray was asleep in his room when, being from L.A., we heard an earthquake. Wood splitting, things breaking. Pennsylvania isn't exactly home to ground-shaking events, so it took me a minute to realize the commotion was Mussolini. He'd busted through the second-floor door, and was on top of Bebi, humping away.

Now I had two pregnant dogs and a lease on a house in Vegas. Debbie was expecting us, and I'd given Candace notice about my job. What could I do? We were gonna have to wait until the puppies were born, then pack everyone and everything into a Penske rental truck. We'd just have to pull the Capri on a trailer behind. We couldn't all fit in that convertible now.

Nine weeks later, Geisha gave birth to seven puppies, and two weeks after that, Bebi had seven more. Our basement was a puppy mill. Stepping over puppies, feeding, watering, and making sure seventeen dogs and two cats had used the bathroom was a full-time job. Ray took over their care while I packed up the rest of the house for our move. It was January in the freezing northeastern corner of Pennsylvania. The weather was god-awful all across the country. What were we thinking?

It never even crossed our minds to adopt the puppies out. We thought we needed to keep them with us for at least four or five months, until they were weaned. We didn't know they could be weaned in a matter of weeks. It also never crossed my mind to take them to the pound. These dogs were my responsibility and I had to step up and care for them.

We built crates into the Penske truck, to keep the puppies from bouncing around, and put the poor cats into crates of their own. Every two to three hours, we had to stop to take the puppies out of the crates, clean them up, and make sure all the dogs and cats and humans were fed, watered, and pooped. At one stop in Tennessee, I returned from the rest stop to find Ray totally overwhelmed. Fourteen puppies were running amok on the rest-stop grounds. Total strangers were chasing them and trying to catch them and help Ray get them back into their crates. I wish I could say the rest of our drive was uneventful, but pretty much every stop turned into a melee.

By the time we got to our house in Vegas, we were exhausted. Debbie came over and helped us unpack. The house was great. The biggest house I'd ever lived in for my entire life. It had a big backyard for the dogs, but I was in over my head. The house was overrun. I was spending more on pet food than I spent on my own groceries, and I wasn't finding easy success breaking into the casino entertainment circuit like I'd hoped.

I took a job working at a pet resort, where rich people "dropped off" their "babies" for some pampering and luxury, instead of sticking them in a kennel during a vacation. The owner of the resort was a dog lover who showed Chows. Working with over a hundred different dogs a day, I learned everything there was to know about dogs. It took me a while to learn their body motions, and what those movements meant, but I watched them closely. I watched how each of the dogs interacted with one another and how each of the breeds seemed to respond in a given situation. The only dogs I couldn't read were Chows. Nothing they did made any sense to me. It took me a long time to understand them.

In my free time, I volunteered for the local NSPCA, helping out at the pound. I learned to become a vet tech, a vet assistant, giving shots, medications, helping the surgeries, doing anything and everything for the dogs. I couldn't stand seeing pit bulls in those cages. I started rescuing dogs one by one, with no thought as to how I'd feed, house, and keep them. I just couldn't stand to see them left there to die.

The pound was a completely different world from the pet resort. It reminded me a lot of going from my childhood in the suburbs to living in the projects. The dogs at the resort had every possible amenity provided for them. The dogs at the pound were forgotten souls, biding their time until they were put down. Country club versus Folsom. I took it personally.

It was my first experience dealing with dog trainers and behaviorists, and it became pretty clear, pretty fucking fast, that any idiot could say they were a dog trainer or a dog behaviorist. Most of them had no idea what they were doing. They'd send people to the pound with dogs that were "unfixable," "untrainable," or "hopeless," which just wasn't true. Any dog is fixable, unless they have a neurological problem. Just like a human. If one trainer isn't able to help, it doesn't mean a dog needs to be euthanized. As far as I'm concerned, I have

a no-kill policy when it comes to all animals. Except tarantulas. I hate tarantulas. You can kill those things if you want.

I was so adamant about my no-kill policy that I even protected a dog that bit me in the face. It happened at the pet
resort. I was the one who handled the pit bulls, 'cause they
were my favorites, and some of the other staff was scared to
handle the breed, regardless of the fact that each dog had an
individual personality. We were short-staffed that day and one
of the girls asked me to get Duke and Daisy out of their pens.
Their owners had arrived and were ready to take them home.

Duke and Daisy were bullmastiffs, big dogs weighing
over a hundred pounds each. They stood over two feet tall, so
we weren't exactly eye to eye, but I only had a couple of feet
and maybe forty pounds up on them. But think about it.
A four-foot-tall, 140-pound guy comes charging at you,
you're probably gonna laugh and take a swing at him. A three-
foot-tall, 120-pound dog comes at you, you might have a different reaction. We humans aren't so efficient at using our
muscle mass the way animals are. That's why I always carry
a bat.

It doesn't mean big dogs are inherently dangerous. Every
dog is a product of its environment. A reflection of its owner.
Bullmastiffs are generally sweet-tempered, but Daisy had
been known to be temperamental. You had to watch out for
her. As I took them out of their pens, I figured I'd handle Daisy
first and get the tough part over with. She started snarling and
showing me her teeth, but I stayed firm and patient with her,
and slowly got her collar around her neck.

I never even saw Duke coming. Next thing I knew, Duke had most of my head in his mouth. He was holding tight and squeezing the shit out of me. I knew I'd be in big trouble if he started to shake me. He was big enough to break my neck. Somehow, I stayed calm. Out of the corner of my eye, I saw a pipe near my foot. They were doing construction on some of the cages and had left materials lying around. I grabbed that pipe and started whacking the shit out of Duke until he let me go.

Before he could decide to take another taste, I rushed out of the holding area and closed the door behind me. I turned around and my coworker took one look at me. She started screaming like a teenager in a horror movie. I didn't realize how much damage Duke had done. I had blood streaming down my face and skin hanging off. I thought she was gonna pass out.

The owners were mortified and panicked that I was gonna report their dogs. I had no intention of reporting Duke. If I did, he would at best be quarantined, and at worst be put down. But the wound was deep, and I needed stitches, so I had to go to urgent care. The owners said to send them the bill, and my coworker drove me. The doctors sewed me up with eight stitches, and when they asked what happened, I told them, "I was out cleaning the roof. I slipped and fell and landed on some barbed wire and got messed up." They knew I'd been bitten by a dog, but I stuck to my story, and Duke and Daisy went safely home.

I wasn't trying to protect my job. I wasn't trying to protect the pet resort. I honestly wasn't mad at Duke for being a dog, and I wasn't gonna be responsible for his demise. A few stitches weren't gonna kill me. I was fine.

It was the first and only time that a dog ever bit me. It never happened again.

■ ■ ■

It was a rough start for us in Vegas. I was booking a few entertainment jobs here and there. An appearance as an elf. A leprechaun. Mini-Me. The work wasn't steady, and I was struggling financially. Allison and I decided to change the name of our company from Short Entertainment to Shortywood, in the hopes we could conjure up some of that Hollywood magic. But mostly, I spent hours hustling to land a gig in Salt Lake City or a gig in Miami. I just couldn't seem to break into the Vegas casino circuit.

Even with the clients that hired me, respect didn't come easy. I worked with a client in Miami to book ten Oompa Loompas for his company's holiday party. We'd been talking by phone for nearly two months, back and forth, to secure the contract, but when I arrived at the hotel, with all ten fully dressed Oompa Loompas and Ray in tow, the client walked up to Ray, shook his hand, and said, "Shorty Rossi, I've been waiting to meet you."

There I was, wearing a suit, with Ray all thugged out and everyone else dressed like a damn Oompa Loompa. I looked at him and said, "I'm Shorty Rossi." The guy laughed in my face.

He could not fathom that I was the one in control. He actually thought 'cause I was Little I must be stupid.

That did it. I said, "You know what, I will eat this one. We're leaving." I loaded up my Oompa Loompas, and assured them they would get paid anyway. The guy totally panicked, but I didn't care. I yelled, "Sue the shit out of me!" And we would have bailed, if he hadn't offered to double our fees as an apology. I might have been offended, but I wasn't an idiot. I took his check and headed back to Vegas, reminded that just 'cause I'd named the company Shortywood didn't mean I was gonna be taken seriously as a real industry player. If I wanted to be seen as a businessman, it wasn't enough to wear the suit, print a card, or even do a good job. I had to fight for every ounce of respect.

Then, to top it all off, Ray got hooked back on crack, and was arrested for possession. He spent a few nights in lockup, tried to clean himself up, slipped again, and ended up back in holding. This went on three or four times, and every time he came back to the house, he promised me it wouldn't happen again. I tried to believe him, but I knew where we were headed.

You can't force an addict to get off it until he is ready. Moving to Vegas had been a big mistake for Ray. I tried to convince him to go back to San Francisco, to be with his family, but he wouldn't go back. I did my best to tolerate the situation, but living with seventeen dogs, two cats, and a crack addict, I was going nuts. After years of being best friends, I had to kick Ray out of my house.

I sat Ray down for a serious talk. "Dude, I've gotta let you go. You're always gonna be a person that was a huge part of my life. We've been together how many years? But I don't need this. I got enough shit going on." It was one of the hardest decisions I'd ever made, but Ray didn't wanna grow up. He wasn't shooting and robbing people anymore, but he just couldn't stay off the pipe. Ray hated me for it. He thought I was the worst man in the world. He moved in with his girlfriend, a woman with five kids, and as far as I know, that's where he stayed.

Ray had been my wingman for years. Without him around, and with Jerry dead, I felt pretty lost. Never mind the practical day-to-day of life with the dogs. Ray and I had always split the responsibility. On my own, I was overwhelmed. I hired a neighborhood kid named Dante to help, and I put the puppies up for sale. I didn't understand that breeding and rescuing were at cross purposes. I thought I could do them both. I took over Ray's room for use as my bedroom, and made the rest of the house a dog sanctuary. Sanctuary is the wrong word. I was hoarding pit bulls.

I had pits in the office. Pits in the extra bedrooms. Pits in the garage. I'd even air-conditioned the garage to keep the pits from roasting in the Nevada heat. I had twenty crates to hold the dogs that still needed to be socialized. The rest of the dogs were loose in the house. At one point, I was up to twenty adult pits and another twenty puppies. There was one puppy, a big guy for such a young pup, who always wanted his way, wouldn't let me out of his sight, but was the single worst puppy I'd ever had. He could tear through drywall like it was rice paper. He'd literally eat through the walls of the house. He drove me insane, but for some reason, I loved him most of all. I named him Hercules.

I was so deep in, I couldn't see the forest for the trees, until Sebastian came to visit. He'd flown out for a couple of nights to work a Shortywood gig, and to hang with me. The minute he walked into my house, he said, "It sounds like a pound in here." I told him, "Stand to the side," as I opened the sliding glass door, walked through the dining room, the living room, the hallway, and opened the dog door. There was a stampede of dogs, charging for the backyard. They all had to pee. Seb's face turned white. He'd never been so scared in his life. He just looked at me. "How can you live with all these dogs?" It was a question I wouldn't dare let myself ask. It was like an addiction. If a rescue group called me, looking for a home for a dog, I took them in. I couldn't say no.

I'd get calls from people in nearby towns. "Come help this dog!" One call led me to a group of pit bulls that had been fought. They'd been left in an abandoned backyard to die. There were five of them, and they were mangled, bleeding, ripped apart. They'd been zapped with electrical prods or stun guns. They'd been beaten and were near death. One of the dogs died in Debbie's arms. There was nothing we could do. I called the vet I worked with at the pound and asked him to come out and put the dogs out of their misery. We couldn't even transport them; they were in such bad shape. How could a human do something like that to an animal? I couldn't understand people. It made me so angry. It was the worst thing I'd ever witnessed and I'd seen a guy disemboweled and hanging from a tier at Folsom.

Another call, a lady from Sutherland, an upscale neighborhood, found a stray pit she couldn't keep. I took the dog in and found it a good home, but the lady wouldn't leave me alone. She wanted to know where I had placed the dog. She wanted to meet the new owners. She wanted to approve of their house. That wasn't my deal. I took a picture of the dog with her new owners in Summerville and gave the lady the photo. It still wasn't enough for her. She accused me of fighting pit bulls. Of using her rescue dog as a bait dog. She threatened to call animal control on me. I told her, "Lady, if that's what you wanna do, then do it, but you will be killing a whole bunch of pit bulls." She never called animal control, but my experience with her, combined with the chaos of my living situation, had really soured me on rescue.

Dog rescue often turns normal, loving, good-intentioned people into crazy fanatics. Rescue can engulf your entire life. It can ruin your relationships with your family and friends. I got a cold, hard look at it there in Vegas. Rescuers filing for bankruptcy 'cause the dogs take every cent. Then there are the rescuers living off their dogs by raising money, and spending it on themselves instead. If you've got a hundred dogs to feed and you're collecting checks on their behalf, then the money should go to the dogs. Not your hair or your nails. How can you have nice nails when you run a facility for dogs? There is no way in hell you don't break a nail every fucking day.

There was a huge rescue organization, and it was common knowledge that they had their own private jet. A jet? With the money they used to maintain the plane, they could have saved a thousand more dogs! People forgot why they started doing what they're doing. There's a big difference between adopting a dog and rescuing a dog. You can rescue all the dogs you want in the world, but if you don't put in the effort to find them homes, you're gonna end up running a pound.

I know, 'cause I was exactly that: a breeder running a pound. I hadn't planned to be. I hadn't thought it out. It never crossed my mind that selling pit puppies was a bad thing, until I started seeing my puppies, months later, all grown up and dropped at the pound. Those tiny guys and gals that I'd brought into the world were now full-grown adult pit bulls on death row. I thought I'd done everything I could to give them good homes, but I'd failed. It was like someone stabbed me in the heart.

I got very opinionated about breeding very fast, and I was vocal about it. I thought every breeder should have to get a state license to breed, and that the license should be goddamn expensive. I thought every breeder should be able to show records of who adopted their dogs for the past ten years, and that their dogs had to be neutered and spayed before adoption. If someone was adopting a dog to show, then they had to provide proof of that career, and they had to sign an agreement not to stud their dog out. If they got caught offering stud services, they would be fined, and the dog would be reclaimed by the original owner. If a breeder found out that a new owner was fighting their pits, then that breeder would have the right to reclaim their dog and turn the owners in to the police. With my big mouth, I spouted my new philosophy wherever I went, and breeders hated me. I didn't care. Those breeders were selling sperm for $500–$1000 a pop, with no thought as to the consequences of their actions.

I was down in the trenches, at the pound, seeing the war on pit bulls and Chihuahuas. Every other cage, pit bull, Chihuahua, pit bull, Chihuahua. It was an endless stream of abandonments, and our pound was just one small building in the middle of Las Vegas. Across the country, pounds were killing thousands and thousands and thousands and thousands of dogs a day. In Los Angeles, the number of dogs being euthanized was so staggering that they couldn't dispose of the carcasses. Their solution? The pounds started rendering the dead dogs and selling their remains to farmers as cow food.

I couldn't turn a blind eye to my own participation in the problem. I adopted back all the pit bulls that made it to the pound, and got all my dogs fixed, except Hercules, who turned out to be allergic to anesthesia. He almost died on the operating table. I resolved to find all my pits good homes and to get out of the rescue and breeding business. There had to be a better way. I just didn't know what it was.

■　■　■

Then, in 2005, Denver reenacted a 1989 citywide policy prohibiting anybody from "owning, possessing, keeping, exercising control over, maintaining, harboring, or selling a pit bull" in the City and County of Denver. They defined a pit bull as any dog that was "an American Pit Bull Terrier, an American Staffordshire Terrier, a Staffordshire Bull Terrier, or any dog displaying the majority of physical traits of any one or more of these breeds." In other words, if your dog was a mutt, but it looked anything like a pit bull, fuck you, we're killing your dog.

Rescue people sent me graphic, horrible photos of dead dogs in barrels. Thousands of pit bulls, put down and thrown into piles like they were the scum of the earth. From puppies to companion dogs that had been with families for twelve, thirteen years, they just rounded them up and slaughtered them. The dogs were annihilated 'cause of their breed, not 'cause they'd done anything wrong. People either had to uproot their families and move out of the city to save their pet's life, or they had to surrender their dogs. It was unbelievable. There was a war being waged against pit bulls, and I felt powerless. I was just some guy in Vegas with a house full of pit bulls. I couldn't do nothing.

Didn't people know that moms used to call pit bulls "nanny" dogs, because they could be left alone with the kids, to watch over them? Pit bulls had been America's sweetheart breed: admired, respected, and loved. They'd been used on propaganda posters for World War I and II, with slogans like "Neutral, but not afraid of any of them" and "We're not looking for trouble, but we're ready for it." Sergeant Stubby, a pit bull, was the most decorated war dog to have served in the U.S. military. In the First World War, he warned troops of incoming attacks. He even captured a German spy all on his own. He was a legend and a hero.

RCA Victor and the Buster Brown Shoe Company used pits as their mascots. A pit named Petey was the star of the Our Gang comedies, better known as *The Little Rascals*. It used to be common knowledge that pit bulls had accompanied pioneer families across the country. Laura Ingalls Wilder, of the popular *Little House* series of books, owned a working farm dog, a pit bull named Jack. Theodore Roosevelt and Helen Keller had even owned pit bulls. So why was Denver outlawing an entire breed? Because pit bulls were ghetto dogs, project pups. Pit bulls were a class issue. A race issue. Ever since states started prosecuting dog fights or animal abuse as felony crimes in the late '70s, the sport had gone underground. It stopped being a pastime of the white elite, and started being the hustle of the drug world, the gang world, the underprivileged. Pit bulls were portrayed as glorified gladiators in every rap video that played on MTV.

The stigma destroyed their sweetheart reputation. They were demonized in the press and they were vilified. The same thing had happened to Chows and Dobermans and German Shepherds in the '70s and early '80s, but now it was pit bulls and Rottweilers that were taking the fall. People turned on their TVs and heard sensationalized stories about pit bull attacks, or kids being mauled, and rather than examine the facts of that particular case, they swallowed the Kool-Aid and became fearful.

The dogs were not designed to kill. They had no special

"enzyme" that made them fight. It's only humans that consciously make the decision to kill. All dogs are capable of violence if they've been trained by shitty owners to be nasty, protective, fighting machines. Owners think that allowing their dogs to bark at or charge a door is protection. They think that dogs naturally know how to be guard dogs. They're too damn lazy to pick up a book and figure out the right way to train their pet. If owners allow dogs to behave badly, they will behave badly. Just like kids.

If some parent isn't paying attention and leaves their kid in the basement with an unneutered male pit bull and a female in heat, there's gonna be trouble. If some gangbanger trains a pit bull to help with a home invasion, and the dog tears into some old lady, I can guaran-damn-tee you it wasn't the dog's idea to break into that house. For God's sake, there was a case in Florida where a Pomeranian mauled a baby to death, but people didn't run out and kill all the Pomeranians. Why were pit bulls being executed?

I'd never felt so powerless in the face of such outright horror. Not in prison, not in the projects, not even at home. If breeding and boarding weren't solutions to the problem, and entire cities were annihilating pit bulls by the thousands, how would I ever be able to make a difference? What was the solution? I had no idea.

■   ■   ■

Amid all this, I decided to go through communion. I'd been baptized Catholic as a baby, but my parents abandoned their traditions sometime during my elementary school years. Church wasn't something that even registered for me during high school. At DeWitt, I'd studied the different religions out of curiosity. I studied the beliefs of Muslims, Seventh-Day Adventists, Jehovah's Witnesses, even the Mormons. Religion intrigued me. I went to Mass a few times at Folsom, but it hadn't taken hold of me the way it took hold of me in Vegas.

I knew I should do it on my own, with nobody else's involvement, with no one pushing me to do it. It wasn't like I wanted to preach at people about the right religion or the right way to live. Every person has to make that choice for themselves. But I'd always believed in a sense of a higher being, even though I personally might never make it to heaven for the things I'd done. Through the years of my life, I hadn't been a saint. I harbored no illusions about my chances for redemption, but learning about the Catholic traditions reminded me of my grandparents. I wanted to feel closer to them. I started a process called the RCIA, the Rite of Christian Initiation of Adults. It was a two-year process to learn more about my faith, my own soul, and to prepare for a period called purification and enlightenment. Since I'd been baptized as a baby, I didn't have to be baptized again, but I still had to be confirmed. On Lent, I received the sacraments of initiation and I officially changed my name.

I'd been going by Shorty since I was in junior high. At Universal, my checks were made out to Shorty Rossi, but that name wasn't on my Social Security card. When I'd done all that genealogical research in prison, I found I had two birth certificates with two different names. One was Melvin Louis Rossi and the other was Melvin Luigi Rossi. When I quizzed Mom about the discrepancy, she said the hospital made a mistake, but she wouldn't tell me which name was the mistake. There was no getting a straight answer from her.

So, in defiance, I said, "Fuck it. I'm gonna change my name." I picked Luigi Francis Shorty Rossi. I added Francis, my communion name, chosen in honor of St. Francis of Assisi, the patron saint of animals. I loved the story about St. Francis and the wolf. There was a legend that when he'd lived in the city of Gubbio, a wolf was terrorizing the town. Francis had gone up in the hills to find the wolf, and when he did, he made the sign of the cross and said, "Brother Wolf, you have done great evil. People accuse and curse you but let us make peace between you and the people." Francis walked the wolf into town and explained to the people that the wolf wasn't evil. He was hungry. If people would feed the wolf, he wouldn't attack them or their animals. Then he blessed the wolf and let him go.

I could relate to Francis and his wolf. It's just that in my life the wolf was a pit bull and every city in America felt like they were under attack. That their kids weren't safe. That the pit bull was evil. How in the world was I gonna come down off a hill and convince people that pit bulls weren't terrorizing people. It was people terrorizing pit bulls.

Would I ever achieve sainthood? Hell, no. Is there a heaven and hell? I'll find out. Which one am I going to? I don't know, but I knew it was important for me to take communion, to change my name, and to be reborn to the world.

■ ■ ■

It took me almost two years to successfully land work in Vegas, but when it rained, it poured. Out of nowhere, I landed three jobs. The first, on the Strip, was a show at the Sahara called Buck Wild. There was a four-hundred-pound drag queen who impersonated Dolly Parton. She'd step out on-stage, wearing this huge hoop-skirt dress, lip-synching the duet "Islands in the Stream." When it was my cue, I'd pop out from under her dress, made up like a mini–Kenny Rogers, and I'd lip-synch the rest of the song with her. The audience always peed their pants. I was a big hit, and it was great money for fifteen minutes of work.

I got a second gig, once a week, in Showtime at the Aladdin, and a third gig in Tiny Kiss, a cover band of Little People dressed as Kiss, for a show I'll call Circus Insanity. Circus Insanity was just that, an insane circus of acts: comics, fire-eaters, glass-walkers, trained monkeys, and contortion-ists, a kind of sideshow, circus, and carnival, presided over by a "Ringleader," played by one of the sleaziest guys in the busi-ness. He was the producer and star, and he hated me. I was his biggest nightmare.

That producer treated his employees terribly, making promises he had no intention of keeping. I rallied all the Little People in the show together and we went on strike. He screamed at me, "You'll never amount to nothing without me. You're a fucking midget!" That was just the motivation I needed.

I walked off his show and formed my own Kiss cover band with Little People. I kicked it into high gear, and got my band booked for every possible gig I could find, and the local papers started covering the "Battle of the Bands" with article headlines screaming, "Who's the Real Tiny Kiss?" In all of those articles, they mentioned Shortywood, and business for Allison and me kicked into high gear. Casting directors from all over the country started calling our offices to hire our talent. It was a good thing too, 'cause Showtime was canceled, then Buck Wild was cancelled, and all of a sudden work went from three shows to nothing. I was right back where I started, working at the doggie spa and volunteering for the pound, trying to make ends meet. I took some gigs wrestling. For some reason, there are people who think it's hilarious to see a bunch of midgets beat the shit out of each other. So beat the shit out of each other we did. We'd hit each other with frying pans, tear at each other with cheese graters, and stab each other with thumbtacks. My character was either the referee or the emcee, but that didn't stop me from ending up under a pile of bodies, or getting slapped upside the head with a baking sheet. There were so many matches where I was thrown through the air and landed flat on my back. I always got up, but after one match, I collapsed. I'd thrown my back out.

I refused to go to the hospital, but found myself there anyway. They did a CAT scan and an MRI, and the doctor showed me all the damage I'd done. This was more than a pulled muscle. All those years of stunts had taken their toll. I had tingling and numbness in my legs, a pinched nerve, sciatica, blah, blah,

blah. It explained why sometimes I'd fall for no reason. I was gonna need physical therapy. I was gonna need major rehab. My performing career was over.

The news hit me like a ton of bricks, but all I could think was, "I miss L.A." Touring everywhere, living in different cities, getting to see everything, I realized L.A. was my comfort zone. I knew the city like the back of my hand. Okay, driving all the time sucked, but L.A. was my home. With my career finished, almost all my dogs adopted out to good homes, and summer approaching, meaning temperatures well over 110 degrees, there was no reason to stay in Vegas.

Packing just wasn't an option. I was in bed for an entire month. The only time I'd make myself walk was to get to the bathroom. Hercules was barely a year old, but he wouldn't leave my side. The monster that ate drywall, the dog that had cost me thousands and thousands of dollars fixing the house, was now my nurse. He refused to let me out of his sight. Geisha could have given a rat's ass. She'd have come in, shit on me, and left, if I'd let her. Mussolini was so big and hyper he would jump onto the bed, not understanding that it caused me pain. Bebi was off in wonderland most of the time, but Hercules had really surprised me. His actions made me think, "There's a bond here."

Debbie kept checking in on me. I still had two too many dogs, so Debbie agreed to take Crash, a goofy pit with the odd habit of crashing into walls headfirst, and I was able to find one last home for a huge, lovable pit named Reno. A group of good friends came over and packed all my things into a

U-Haul, while I pretty much lay there like a stone. I wasn't driving to L.A. yet. I was heading to San Francisco for specialized rehab for my back.

■ ■ ■

It was my doctor in San Francisco who first suggested I get a service animal. I believe his direct quote was, "You've got all those damn pit bulls. Why not train one of them to help you?" I had no idea where to start. The doctor actually wrote me a prescription for a service animal, and instructed me to go to the animal shelter and get a "service dog in training" tag and kit. I did as he said, then realized I had a lot of reading to do to figure this out.

Depending on the nature of a disability, a person is assigned a certain kind of animal. If I'd been blind or deaf, I'd have had to get a dog that had been through service animal college. If I'd had seizures, or needed a dog that could signal a diabetic attack, I'd have had to purchase a specially trained dog. My prescription was for mobility. I needed a dog that could pull me upstairs, carry my things, function as a leg rest when I was seated, keep me from falling, or if I did fall, help me up. Basically, act as a sentient, powerful cane. There were classes I could attend to help with mobility training but I decided I'd read all the books myself and give it a shot.

Geisha seemed like the best option. She was friendly with people, calm in her demeanor, and she was my first girl. I was very attached to her. I took her everywhere I went anyway. Why not throw the service dog vest on her and call it a day?

She turned out to be a handful. She started growling at passing dogs. Geisha was older and was getting set in her ways, like an old, grumpy lady. She wasn't interested in toting me around.

So I gave Hercules his shot. He'd never been out in public, but ever since my back injury, he'd been attached to my hip, so I figured I'd take him out for a test drive. I wanted to visit a friend in Stockton. I loaded Hercules up with a harness bag that held my laptop computer and all my crap, then we headed out to get on the BART. It was rush hour, and the train was loaded with people, but Hercules didn't even flinch. He pulled me up the stairs, got me settled into a seat, and then lay down by my feet. I couldn't believe how docile he was. He was just happy to be with me. Happy to do his job. He instinctively knew what I needed. From that point on, Hercules became my right-hand man.

I never thought I'd own a handicapped parking placard. I always considered them a fraud. Every Little Person I knew had one, but only fifteen percent of them really needed it. Little People used them selectively. If they were with someone tall, they wouldn't use them, 'cause they'd be ashamed, but if they were by themselves or with another Little Person, you better believe they'd whip those babies out and take the closest space. Now that I couldn't walk long distances, I finally gave in and got the permit, and what a difference to be able to park so close! I wished I'd had the damn thing for the last ten years.

I didn't feel sorry for myself, and I didn't regret any of the stunts or wrestling jobs or abuse I had put my body through for the last six years. I wasn't worried about my future, and I wasn't gonna let my back injury slow me down. No one knows how long they're gonna live, and I wasn't gonna spend the time I had worrying about my health when I could die in a car wreck or on a damn airplane the next morning. Frankly, a fiery crash was preferable to liver cancer or lung cancer or diabetes.

That's why I got the bright idea that if I bought a pair of tennis shoes with wheels built in to the bottoms, then Hercules could pull me faster. In theory, this was a smart idea. In practice, it was a disaster waiting to happen. Wheels on your shoes in hilly San Francisco seemed like fun, until I realized I had no idea how to use the damn things. I got the wheels out and moving, and Hercules was like, "Oh, this is so much easier." He took off at a trot. Then a run. Bam! Right into a lamppost. So much for my bright idea.

I was feeling much better, but there was still back pain every day. The doctor told me to change my diet, stop smoking and drinking, stop working so much, and lower my stress level, but none of that was actually gonna happen. I'm a workaholic. An adrenaline junkie. I wanted to experience a full life, even if it meant I ended up in a wheelchair, and even that wouldn't stop me. I could hook up my dogs and they could pull it like a sleigh.

Fuck, I already had the damn elf costume to match!

8

Pimpin'

Shortywood had never been a full-time job for either me or Allison. For the most part, it had been the equivalent of bonus cash. It was money we couldn't rely on, but appreciated when it showed up. Before my injury, my primary paychecks came from performing, but for Allison, she made her money in Orange County real estate.

By the time I got back to Los Angeles in 2007, the city was in the grip of a real estate frenzy at the same time that Shortywood was really taking off. We now had about two hundred Little People around the world on our talent roster, and job calls were happening every week. Allison was living with her boyfriend down in Orange County, and her real estate job had become more than a backup—it was lucrative. She kept trying to do both, but it was just too much work and travel. We talked it through, and it dawned on me: Allison was leaving Shortywood.

Allison and I had built the company together. I'd relied

on her heavily to keep the business from falling apart while I was on the road, and she'd been a great partner. She was a hard worker and always responsible. It was hard to lose her. She wasn't gonna be easy to replace, but there was no way I could handle everything by myself. With my dancing and acting career completely kaput, Shortywood was my bread and butter. It was my sole source of income. It had to be a success. I had no backup plan. And now there was overhead. All those costumes that lived in Allison's house had to live somewhere. I rented an office in Hollywood, and Shortywood went from being a two-page website with a cell phone to a full-fledged management office. I had my own desk. I could put my feet up on it if I damn well pleased. Finally, after decades of dreaming about being a boss, I was the boss!

Only sixty percent of my time was spent managing talent. The other forty percent of my day was spent operating a pit bull rescue. Essentially, I functioned like a transport system for pit bulls, picking them up from rescue shelters, pounds, abandoned buildings, or running wild on the streets, and finding them homes. I was resolved not to become a boarding facility for any reason. I wasn't gonna repeat the mistakes I made in Vegas, but I still wanted to be of service to these dogs.

Pit bulls were back on the front page of the news. Atlanta Falcons quarterback Michael Vick was arrested for owning and operating a competitive dogfighting ring called the Bad Newz Kennels, which fought dogs across several state lines. Police had removed over sixty dogs from his property in Virginia, where they found bloodstains on the walls of a room, and a bloodstained carpet. The house was actually customized for dog fights. It had a high fence to keep people from seeing what was going on, and a bunch of sheds where the dogs were trained, or where injured dogs were left. Vick had executed eight dogs himself, by hanging, drowning, and slamming one dog's body to the ground. He was also a registered dog breeder.

Oh my God, was I pissed. Michael Vick may have grown up in the projects, but once he went to college, he should've learned his lesson. And once he became an NFL superstar, he should've known that killing dogs was wrong. There was no excuse for it. He deserved to lose everything he'd worked so hard to accomplish. All the endorsement deals and the admiration of his fans, I was glad to watch it all crumble down around his feet. The media wouldn't let the story go, and as hard as it was to hear the details, Michael Vick's downfall was shining a light on a major problem for pits. The cruelty was astounding. It shocked the public out of their ignorance. For that, I was happy. For those sixty-plus dogs that had suffered, I wanted Vick in jail.

For me to say Vick needed to do time, I had to be steaming mad. And by doing time, I meant they should throw him in the hole. No TV, no radio, no special food requests, no gym access, no day for day. If you're gonna punish somebody, then punish them and enforce the education programs. Make them mandatory. Guys need to be taught right from wrong so they will understand what they've done and not do it again. Sitting around all day, working an easy job, and having all your meals provided for you doesn't teach you nothing. Believe me, I know. All you learn is how to be a smarter, better criminal. We'd be better off as a society if most of these guys had to do service as punishment instead of time. They'd learn more and have to work harder to pay their debts. Could Michael Vick come out of prison a changed man? Yes, he could. I was walking proof that reform is possible. Would he be a forgiven man? Not by Shorty.

Vick's actions caused a huge spike in phone calls to my office, of people reporting pit bulls and bait dogs being used in fights. Suddenly, people felt more empowered to speak up on behalf of injured dogs, even if they weren't willing to adopt the dogs themselves. We were so overloaded with calls, I couldn't juggle both jobs and keep Shortywood profitable, so I asked Sebastian if he'd help me out in the office. He'd been going on gigs for me for years and he wasn't one of the Little fucks who complained all the time. If I booked him, he showed up and did the work. Maybe it was his high school years as a wrestler that gave him the discipline and work ethic I respected. Whatever, we got along. I also knew he was a better organizer than I was. Anal-retentive is a better term. Seb always did things by the book. He seemed like the right choice.

Seb came on board working as my second in command. Once I handled the financial part of a deal, Seb would take over and handle the logistical details, making sure things ran smoothly. He also brought Ronald, my old roommate from the Radio City Tour, into the mix. He and Ronald had become good friends over the years. Ronald functioned as our booking assistant, confirming the talent, arranging travel for out-of-town events, organizing the costumes, hair, and makeup. He still drove me crazy with his lateness, but Seb stayed on top of him and made sure the work got done.

I hired a receptionist as well, a girl named Ashley Brooks. Her girlfriend, Kacie, normally worked for me at the desk, but Kacie was busier and busier with stunt-double work, so Ashley filled in. She was new to the business. She'd done her first gig for Shortywood in Salt Lake City, playing Snow White—with the Seven Dwarves—for a computer company. She was so spunky. I had to calm her down. She wasn't a diva. She didn't care if she had to wear a costume for a job. She never complained that the work was "degrading" like Ronald did. She'd just jump in and get it done.

The only problem was that she was scared to death of the dogs. I told her, "Dogs come with the job. Take your pick." There was really no way to avoid it. Bebi, Mussolini, Geisha, and Hercules were always with me. Bebi and Mussolini actually lived at the office, since the landlord of my Hollywood apartment would allow me to keep only two dogs, Geisha and Hercules, at home. It wasn't an ideal situation by any means. I wanted all my dogs with me at all times, but for now, it was the compromise I had to make. Ashley was fragile at first, but after a while, she'd get knocked down by a dog and she'd just jump right back up, ready to go.

None of them knew that by taking the job with Shortywood, they'd also signed themselves up for full-time pit bull rescue. As pit bull rescue became a bigger part of the operation, Seb took on more responsibility, going on rescues with me and helping find foster and permanent homes for the pups and strays. Ronald got interested in how to train pit bulls for entertainment jobs and learned how to socialize the dogs in preparation for adoption. We all started going to pit bull awareness events as a team. Everywhere we went, we turned heads. Three or four midgets and four pit bulls showing up to learn more about breed-specific legislation . . . we weren't their typical audience members.

Fighting against BSL, breed-specific legislation, was the movement I'd been searching for, the missing piece of the puzzle. This is how we could save the breed. I could focus on advocacy instead of rescue. I could raise awareness in order to protect pit bulls from abusive, restrictive legislation simply by going out there, every day, and letting people know what type of dog a pit bull really is. I could see the surprise on people's faces when they saw Hercules as my service dog. They were shocked to see a docile, sweet pit bull by my side.

I could reach out to communities that were being ignored. Pit bulls are project dogs and 'cause I was from the projects, and 'cause I had street cred and Folsom years behind me, these guys would listen to me. I could get them to at least consider the free spay and neuter program provided by the City of Los Angeles. There was no way to force these guys to do the right thing. People only change when they're ready to change, whether it's fighting addiction or fighting dogs. But I could be a voice, letting these guys know: actually, no, it's not cool to breed dogs. That one litter can become a puppy mill in the blink of an eye. That no, it's not cool to fight your dog. That it's greed and cruelty, plain and simple.

It's not about screaming at some twenty-year-old kid, and telling them they're stupid or dumb to be doing what they're doing. You'll just make them more violent. You just show them something different. A different way of thinking. A different way of seeing. The younger you catch them, the better off you are. Whenever we'd visit the junior highs with Geisha or Hercules, I could see the kids "get it," but to really be effective, I needed to find some way to reach people, both kids and adults, in bigger numbers. One-on-one pit bull rescue was like sticking my chubby finger in a leaking Hoover Dam. I needed to reach thousands of people, no, millions of people, no, the whole goddamn world and let them know: PIT BULLS ARE NOT THE ENEMY. WE ARE THE ENEMY!

It didn't take long for me to get my chance.

■　■　■

David Coulter, a journalist from the *L.A. Times,* had seen all those articles about Tiny Kiss, and wanted to profile Shortywood for his monthly column on interesting or unusual businesses in the city. We met and spoke at the Hollywood office, then he came to one of our gigs in Newport Beach, where my Little Village People were performing. The article ran in the Business section of the *Times* on March 17, 2007. It was called "For These Performers, No Role Is Too

Small," and it featured a photo of my talent onstage, in costume, dancing in all their glory. The response was immediate. Reality TV production companies and networks were knocking down the door, trying to get hold of us. My calendar filled with dates for my "couch and bottled water" tour. Every time I walked into a meeting, they handed me a bottle of water and showed me the couch.

Hercules and Geisha were with me for all the meetings, and their presence made it obvious who I could work with and who I'd show the door. There were companies that were terrified of my dogs. They didn't want them in the offices. They had no idea I was running a pit bull rescue operation at the same time, and they weren't interested.

But there were two companies I liked, and they started fighting for the rights to shoot a Shortywood pilot. The first was Jay James from E! Network, and the other was Rick Leed, who was then at Frameless Entertainment. Rick had been the executive producer of Tim Allen's *Home Improvement*. Jay wanted to film a five-minute teaser to convince the E! executives to invest in a full pilot. Frameless Entertainment wanted to film enough to present three or four episodes to several different networks, and they didn't require a contract. It seemed like a no-brainer to me. I told the E! Network to go to hell, and started shooting with Frameless.

The pilot was called *Shortywood*, and since we filmed inside my office, the dogs were part of the pilot, even though they weren't the main focus of attention. Domenico and Valentino weren't even around yet, but Geisha and Hercules got plenty of screen time. Once the pilot was done, Rick and I went to every network to pitch the show. Doors slammed one after the other after the other after the other. They were saying things like, "There's already a Little Person reality show on TV."

They were referring to TLC's *Little People, Big World* series that followed the Roloff family on their pumpkin farm. I'd make my case: "Those guys are Ozzie and Harriet. We're the Connors!" But the execs weren't interested. In their minds, one show about Little People was enough. There wasn't room for us. Rick and I pounded the pavement for six months, then we gave up. It wasn't meant to be.

I just kept on with my own business, running Shortywood and the rescue transport system. In the meantime, I tried to find a living situation where I could keep all my dogs together. A friend suggested I rent a house in Big Bear, and commute back and forth. It was a crazy, asinine idea, but for some reason, I agreed to give it a try. I gave up my Hollywood apartment, bought a huge Dodge Ram truck, and drove the dogs out to Big Bear.

The house was great, and the dogs loved the freedom of having a big backyard again, but driving for hours was hell on my back, and getting into that truck only made it worse. The only good thing to come out of the move was adding Domenico to our family. A neighbor had seen a black pit bull with a small head running loose in the woods. I tromped back there to find him, and he was friendly enough to follow me home. I tried to place him with two different families, but he was an escape artist. He just kept breaking away. He wanted to run free. The only time he wouldn't run away was with me. So I kept him.

I barely lasted four months in Big Bear before I packed everyone up again and headed south to Marina del Rey. I rented a houseboat, and divvied the dogs up again between the office and the boat. It wasn't ideal, but finding an apartment that would allow five pit bulls was impossible. Then another friend suggested I consider Mexico. After Big Bear being a bust, I wasn't as quick to start packing my suitcases, but I drove down and took a look. I found a house with a beach view, solid concrete walls, two bedrooms, two levels, for $600 a month. The kicker: no dog laws, nothing. If I wanted all my dogs around me, I could have them. If the neighbors didn't like it, too bad, they could go to hell. Mexico was live and let live. Family-oriented. Big meals, socializing, music, and celebrations. Mexico was my kind of place. I rented the house, but kept my houseboat in the Marina just in case.

Around this time, Animal Planet put out the word that they wanted "edgier" programming. There was a woman named Mechelle Collins who owned a production company called Intuitive Entertainment. She'd seen the pilot Rick and I had shot, and she'd kept us in the back of her mind for almost a year. When she heard that Animal Planet was going edgy, she hunted me down.

She convinced me to give the reality TV series one more try. Only this time, she wanted to focus on the dogs, and not the talent management company. This was exactly the platform I needed to launch a real advocacy campaign for pit bulls! The more we talked, the more excited I got about the idea, but I'd been through this process before and I knew better than to get my hopes up. I agreed to shoot a five-minute teaser for them to take to Animal Planet, but this time I wanted to get out of the office and shoot an actual dog rescue. Mechelle agreed.

She got the teaser DVD to Animal Planet. Once a month, the development team met with the president, Marjorie Kaplan, to look over submissions, and a girl named Hilary popped the DVD into the projector. She basically prefaced it by saying, "Big dogs, Little People." Apparently, everyone in the room was like, "Are you serious? Is this real? Is this a completely staged show? This can't be real. No way in hell."

Animal Planet called Mechelle in disbelief. She told them, "Just Google Shorty Rossi. He's been doing this for years. He's not a fake." So they researched me, and found all the information about Shortywood and the rescue program. They checked out my criminal past and verified my whole history. They realized it wasn't a setup. I may have been an actor in my past career, but I wasn't acting now. With or without a show, Shortywood and Shorty's Recue would continue.

Animal Planet asked to see a full thirty-minute pilot, so Intuitive geared up and we prepped for production. Then Animal Planet called back before we'd even shot a scene and said, "Go ahead and shoot enough material for five or six episodes." What??? It'd barely been two weeks since we sent them the DVD and the contracts were still flying from office to office, unsigned. Then Animal Planet called again and said, "Shoot the full six and we'll air them." We hadn't even shot the pilot yet, and suddenly, I had a guaranteed six-episode pickup to air on Animal Planet.

I refused to believe that any of it was really gonna happen. Even though I was sitting in front of the cameras, and there were people running in and out of my office on a daily basis, I just kept hearing this loop running through my head: "This isn't true. This can't possibly be true." I thought, "Well, they'll shoot the pilot, look at it, and hate it, and cancel the whole deal." Or I thought, "Okay, maybe we'll get six episodes but they'll never show them." Or I thought, "They're gonna decide an ex-con and pit bulls shouldn't be on TV and back out." But they didn't. The show just kept moving forward, and they even set a date for our premiere. January 2010. The show would be called *Pit Boss*.

That's when I almost blew it.

■ ■ ■

Two days before the premiere of the show, the very first episode, Shortywood was hired to do another event in Newport Beach. They wanted the Little Village People for an encore performance, so I drove down, and Allison joined me there. It wasn't so far from her house. It was good to see her, and she liked helping out with the odd job here and there. We always had a good time working together.

I had way too much wine, and I was staying at a hotel nearby, but I heard about an after-party, and decided to go. I threw Hercules back into the Scion, and we were halfway there when I had to make a left turn at a light. I was on the phone, talking to somebody, when I noticed the car opposite me also trying to make a left turn. He was a foot over the double yellow line, but I was tipsy and not paying attention. Between the phone and the booze, I was distracted.

We ran right into each other. My tire blew and his headlight busted. Within two minutes, the cops showed up. My mind was racing. "How am I gonna get out of this?" Given my past record, I just didn't like dealing with cops, ever. I didn't realize I was drunk. I didn't realize the other driver was also drunk. I thought I was sober enough to drive.

The cops asked me how much I'd had to drink. I explained that I was wobbling 'cause I was bowlegged and disabled, not 'cause of the wine. The cop just smiled at me, and said, "Just blow into this thing and get it over with." I blew four points over the legal limit. The cop said, "We gotta take you in." His partner, a lady cop, announced she was gonna call animal control. I almost lost my mind. It took every ounce of energy in me not to freak out. I knew I had to be cooperative. I knew I couldn't piss them off. I was in the wrong, but they were not gonna take Hercules away from me. I convinced the lady that Hercules was my service animal for my disability, and that it could be seen as discrimination if he wasn't allowed to travel with me. She gave me the leash and they loaded Hercules and me into the back of the patrol car. We were quite the sight.

Once we got to booking, they had no idea what to do with Hercules. They put him in a holding cell by himself, where he howled and moaned to be reunited with me. Poor Hercules, behind bars. We'd been captured as part of a DUI sting, so the place was filling up with drunks. The guy sitting beside me was so confused. He kept leaning over to me and saying, "Did they bring us to a dog pound? I'm not hearing a dog in prison, am I? Man, I gotta stop drinking."

I sat there for several hours before a cop came to let me go. He actually said, "You've been so cooperative and you've never been in trouble, so call someone to pick you up." They didn't realize I'd been in prison before. Maybe my name change had confused things a bit. Whatever the reason, I kept my mouth shut, called one of the Little People working the event, Tonya, and had her drive Hercules and me back to the hotel. Four hours later, I called a taxi to take me to the impound yard to get my car. I had to change the tire before I could even drive off the lot.

I was worried I had put Mechelle and Intuitive in a tight spot. I was convinced it was gonna ruin my whole career before it even got off the ground. I couldn't keep the DUI a secret from them. It could all go wrong when we were so close to making it to air. And more than that, I worried that I'd just blown the one opportunity I had to really make a difference for pit bulls. But I had to tell Intuitive. It was the right thing to do. To their credit, Intuitive didn't blow up on me. We all had a lot riding on the success of the show, but more than that, they wanted to make sure I wasn't pulling a Lindsay Lohan, and trashing my career out of some sort of self-sabotage. I let Mechelle know, "It won't happen again. I've learned my lesson."

I had learned my lesson, although I was surprised it took

me until I was almost forty-one to learn it. There were times when I had been so shit-faced coming home from a gig in Vegas that I'd find myself driving down the wrong side of the street; one time, I ended up at the Hoover Dam for no apparent reason. It really made me think. What right did I have to drink and drive? Absolutely none. If I was gonna drive, it would have to be one drink, then stop. If I wanted to party, then I'd just have to fork over the sixty-dollar cab fare to get home, and not bitch about it. Sixty bucks would have saved me a fortune. When all was said and done with the legal fees and fines, that one lousy night out cost me over fifteen grand. More than that, I was lucky no one got hurt. I wasn't gonna press my luck anymore.

Two days later, *Pit Boss,* episode one, aired. They'd been promoting the show heavily, but I was still guarding my hopes against disappointment. When I watched the show, all I could think was, "We got on the air, it'll go for the six episodes and that's it. But we achieved it. I get another notch on my belt to say I did that. Now I can move onto something else." I had no idea what had just happened.

Episode one hit the ratings clean. Then the second episode's numbers came in even higher. Before the third episode even aired, I got called into the Intuitive office. "They are renewing you." Animal Planet had ordered another eight episodes to fill out the first season. It just blew up. Overnight. We went from being nobodies to somebodies. I had no idea so many people watched Animal Planet. People started recognizing me in the streets, yelling, "Pit Boss!"

We thought we were busy before. We hadn't seen the half of it. Little People that hated me were now anxious to be my friend. The number of Little People wanting to be repped by Shortywood doubled. Client calls doubled, if not tripled. I had to institute a new policy about the size of the jobs. They had to be big parties, major blowouts, with big commissions attached. We just couldn't handle the smaller gigs anymore. We didn't have the manpower.

We went from a small operation that only Los Angeles rescue groups knew about to a rescue that was now being recognized across the United States. Our rescue got so big, we couldn't afford it. Taking care of the dogs, helping people adopt the dogs, donating money to different rescue groups, arranging for dogs to get their shots, to be spayed and neutered. It was too much. We were used to handling fifty e-mails and calls a day, between both the entertainment requests and pit bull rescues. The numbers went up to one thousand e-mails and calls a day. It got so crazy, we had to shut down the pit bull rescue line, no longer answer the entertainment line at all, hire some temporary help, and delegate, delegate, delegate. We needed a reality check. I sat my team down and said, "Guys, we gotta do something else. We need more income coming in. This show is gonna bankrupt us!"

People think 'cause you're on TV you must be rich. They don't understand reality TV pay. Life was better, hell yeah, much better, don't get me wrong, but my personal expenses went way, way up. My life had to change. I had to move off the boat and into an apartment with more security features, an extra bedroom for the dogs. It wasn't a luxury situation by any means. My furniture was still IKEA. My neighbors weren't celebrities, but there was a bit more privacy.

Privacy was getting harder and harder to come by, and for a Little Person, that's saying something. There has never been a day when I could move through the world anonymously. I have always been looked at, stared at, noticed. For so many years, I just ignored it. I didn't like to complain about it like other Little People would. If my friends would ask, "Why is everyone staring at you?" I'd just point out the obvious. "'Cause I'm a fucking midget with a pit bull, why do you think?"

Once *Pit Boss* started airing, I was stared at for a completely different reason. I was recognized as a TV personality, and whatever limited anonymity I had left was completely gone. That was fine. That was the life I chose. I knew that to be an advocate for the dogs, I had to step in front of the cameras and give the people a show. I knew that by doing this, the sacrifice was privacy. This time, I knew when people were staring at me, it was 'cause of *Pit Boss*, and not 'cause I was a fucking midget with a pit bull.

But I hadn't really thought it through. I was grateful for the fans, excited to be reaching so many people, but I didn't realize I wouldn't be able to shop at Walmart or Target anymore. I couldn't go to my usual grocery store, Trader Joe's, or if I needed toiletries, I couldn't just swing by the CVS. An errand that used to take me ten or fifteen minutes would turn into a forty-five-minute ordeal with photographs and autographs and people stopping me to talk about their dogs.

Then there were the death threats, the critics, and the cra-
zies. There were people angry that I promoted a "killer" breed.
They blasted me with e-mails, letters, and phone calls, calling me every name in the book, telling me to never set foot
in their city with my dogs 'cause they'd slaughter us all. I was
actually attacked by a hysterical drunk woman who slapped
me across the face three times, screaming that Hercules was
a killer and that he shouldn't be allowed into restaurants.
There were breeders that said my stance against breeding pit
bulls was gonna "wipe out the breed." They considered me an
enemy, not an advocate. There were people running rescue
organizations that were mad at me 'cause I couldn't personally help them place a dog or give them money or show up at
their events. They'd cuss me out and yell, "I'll never watch your
show again." There were people who thought I was a fraud.
People posting nasty things about me online. People flooding my inbox with requests to help a pit bull in Maine, when I
lived in California. Sending me the same e-mail over and over
and over again. For as much love as we got from fans, we got
an equal amount of craziness and hatred.

What was hardest of all was stopping my weekly visits
to the projects. There were old enemies, and even some old
friends, who were jealous of the success of the show. I'd seen
guys who'd made good come back to the projects and get
jumped or robbed. I didn't want to end up like Jerry. I couldn't
let that happen. I couldn't get caught hanging out with guys
who were still selling drugs or robbing people. If a bust went
down and I was standing there, it would destroy my repu-

tation and the show. There were kids out there watching my show, kids who were being inspired to help animals, kids who were writing in and donating their allowances to save pit bulls. I couldn't do nothing to lose their trust. I had to pay closer attention to my circle of friends. I had to stop clubbing and partying in public, where every single person is carrying a cell phone with a camera built in. The show was a monster. That was a good thing. It just meant my life had to change.

It also meant the business had to change. For years, Shorty-wood had been funding the rescue operations, but now the whole operation had flipped on its head. I was adamant that we were not gonna live off the popularity of my dogs. The whole point of rescuing pit bulls was to help the dogs, not use them. Still, we needed some way to raise income to keep up with the new demands. *Pit Boss* had brought us a platform, a way to reach people, but we couldn't rely on donations. We weren't even a nonprofit. We were a glorified transport system!

I don't remember who came up with the idea, but the solution seemed to be opening an online store, Shorty's Store, where we could sell stuff and use the profits to help cover our rescue operation expenses and fund four charities, three of which we'd been working with for years: Furbaby, Karma Rescue, and the Linda Blair Worldheart Foundation. The Watts Youth Foundation was basically defunct now. It had fizzled out during my travels, though now that I was back in Los Angeles, I'd grab some kids from the projects and take them to Universal or the beach. That was on my own dime. With my recent rental in Mexico, I'd also started volunteering at the

Door of Faith Orphanage in Baja. I wanted to include them in our charitable giving. Kids and dogs, both were okay by me. So the decision was made. We'd open an online store. We'd sell things like a Hercules bobble head, dog collars, T-shirts, tote bags, coffee mugs, key rings. Where we were gonna get this stuff or store this stuff was a completely different issue. The office was already packed with people, dogs, and costumes, so the only option was my apartment. The dogs would share my bedroom with me and I'd turn the extra room into storage for the store.

I hadn't anticipated endorsement deals. The first offer came from a company that wanted me to promote their substitute nicotine chewing gum. I told the guy, "You realize I smoke, right?" He said, "Yes, but you could encourage people to stop smoking." I am many things, but a hypocrite is not one. I wasn't gonna take money from a company, lecture people about smoking, and then turn around and have a cigar. Even if those checks would support the dogs, the answer was no.

Then I got a personal invitation from Diesel cigar maker A. J. Fernandez to visit his cigar factory in Nicaragua. He wanted me to come down and check out the factory, the farms, and the tobacco-processing facilities. If all went well, I'd put my name on a cigar. Ten percent of the proceeds would go to Shorty's Charities and I'd get to smoke a bunch of cigars. No-brainer. I was on the plane.

I got to the factory and there were probably a good five hundred people there rolling cigars. The management team, A.J., Alex, and Kris, gave me the grand tour, explaining how the business was run, how cigars are rolled, what kind of tobacco is used, how the wrapper came from Pennsylvania, but the filler was grown in Nicaragua. They sat me down at a workstation and showed me how to roll a cigar. I was given the royal treatment.

The whole time, I could tell that every eye in that factory was on me. One thousand eyeballs staring right at me. It was weird. I wasn't sure what to make of it. Yes, I was used to people peeking out of the corners of their eyes to watch me, but not full out staring, and not five hundred people at the same time. Finally, one of the managers came over to talk to one of the owners. He asked, "Everyone wants to know. They have a question. Please forgive us for being rude, but why are you, the owners, kissing this peasant's ass?"

Whoa.

In most Central American countries, a Little Person is always the peasant. They're poor. They're a circus act. They're marginalized. They're a pariah. They certainly aren't on TV, and they're not doctors or lawyers or teachers or even factory workers. They have no status at all. They are non-people. For me to have an entourage, for the owners of their company to treat me as someone important, seemed ludicrous to them. The owners explained to the manager, "Mr. Rossi is an American businessman. He owns a business and he is on a TV show." The manager went back to give this new information to the workers, but they were completely baffled. They just couldn't understand it. How could a Little Person own a business? Why would a Little Person be on TV?

I had never experienced outright prejudice in such a blatant, in-my-face kind of way. I didn't blame the workers. They'd never seen anyone like me. It made me understand how far we've come, as Little People, to redefine what is possible. The discrimination that my father faced in Texas. The stares that Nonnie, Mom, and me had ignored our whole lives. That was nothing. There were Little People in Nicaragua who were peasants, PEASANTS, 'cause they'd been born small.

Even further back, during World War II, Hitler massacred all the Little People. Only one family survived. A family of seven musical entertainers and only 'cause the Führer himself had a fetish for Snow White and the Seven Dwarfs. Too bad his fetish didn't stop them from being tortured and put through medical testing. In the Middle Ages, my people were court jesters, if they were lucky. If they weren't lucky, they were . . . well, peasants.

Me, I'd grown up knowing I could be anything I wanted to be. It may have taken me twenty goddamn years to get my shit together, but eventually, I'd ended up the businessman I'd always said I'd be. I never let my size determine the size of my life. I was never afraid to become bigger and better, to push myself to jump off a building or start my own company. If you're standing in the way, I'm gonna knock you over, no matter how big you are, so I can get to where I'm trying to go. Move, excuse me! Move! If that's how you look at life, no matter how big or small you are, then you are gonna succeed. You don't let nothing stop you.

Those factory workers were blown away, and on my next visit, everything was different. The managers put American satellite TV in the work breakrooms to show the workers *Pit Boss* episodes. *Pit Boss* posters were all over the walls, and as soon as I walked in, a girl came up to me and said in Spanish, "I just finished rolling one of your own cigars. It's an honor for you to smoke this one."

Minds had changed in Nicaragua.

- - -

Meanwhile, what was supposed to be a three-month program of classes to rectify my DUI dragged on and on, as I had to keep taking leave to shoot episodes, to rescue a dog, or to travel for personal appearances. It didn't help that I got kicked out of class twice for running my big mouth. The first teacher and I couldn't get along. She was of the mentality that anyone in her class was going to hell for drinking. She made us raise our hands if we'd had a drink in the last twenty-four hours. I raised my hand. She looked at me. "What are you gonna do about your problem?" I yelled, "Problem? I had a glass of wine. I deal with goddamn Little People all day!" . . . You may leave the class.

Her next session, I got tossed out 'cause she put on an *Intervention* video about a girl who was cutting herself. Even after being in prison, and seeing all that horrifying stuff, blood made me squeamish. Homies used to tease me about it, but I'd rather be freaked by blood than numb. I yelled out in the middle of class, "Why are we watching this suicidal blood shit when we're a bunch of drunks?" . . . You may leave the class, part two.

Fortunately, for my third class, I had a new teacher. He'd been a former addict, a gang member, and he'd done time, so I could relate. He recognized me from *Pit Boss*, so like anyone else who'd ever watched the show, he knew my backstory, knew I'd done time at Folsom. We reminisced about the CDC, shot the shit about our numbers, the Level 4's, and things only guys from prison would understand. His name was Robert and he was a good guy, clean and sober, determined to stay out of jail.

What struck me most about his class was all the people in those seats. There were old people, young people, three-time offenders, and first-timers. Every ethnicity, every gender, every race, size, color, and type. So many people. The size and scope of the problem seemed enormous, and the secrecy and the shame surrounding it only made matters worse. Instead of fessing up and admitting, "Yeah, I blew it. I won't ever do that again," people kind of retreated into themselves, ashamed and feeling even worse about their lives. Which just seemed like a recipe for more of the same. Robert's honesty about his own criminal past helped get people talking. Hearing their stories was . . . well, sobering.

When I finished my last class, Robert pulled me aside and said, "You're smarter than this, Shorty. I know I won't see you again." He was right. I had a lot to lose, and I wasn't gonna lose it over a drink. I wasn't proud of what I'd done, but I took it as another lesson of my life. Was I an alcoholic? Maybe. If I was, I was a high-functioning one. Would I have another drink? Definitely. Would I drive after that drink? Definitely not.

There were bigger battles I needed to fight, and just like I wouldn't allow my father, my childhood, the projects, my arrest, prison, financial struggles, or Ray struggling with crack or losing Jerry or being fired from jobs or having back pain to get in my way, I wasn't gonna allow this DUI to sidetrack me from my larger mission. To this day, I have no regrets about any of my mistakes. I wouldn't change a thing, which must seem crazy to most people, but is true for me. It's not that I don't regret some of my actions. I do. But if I hadn't run away, if I hadn't gotten in trouble, if I hadn't been arrested, I'd definitely be dead. Being in prison made me the man I am today. Most men don't come through those years and improve their lives, but I did. It made a difference to me. I was reformed. I'm a better, bigger man 'cause of those years. I knew that the DUI was another part of forging me into a stronger, more determined warrior.

The problem with me was still when I heard the word "no" I wouldn't listen. If someone said, "You shouldn't do that" then that was exactly what I was gonna do. It made me arrogant and cocky, but it also made me the Pit Boss. It made me Shorty Rossi. It was exactly that combination of arrogance and cockiness and sometimes idiocy that caused people to tune in to *Pit Boss*. By having Hercules and Geisha and Bebi and the rest of my pits on the show, we were changing people's minds about the breed. By traveling from city to city with Hercules by my side, working as my service animal, we were changing airline, airport, restaurant, and hotel policies. Celebrity allowed me to bend the rules, setting a new precedent for other disabled people who might consider adopting a pit bull, for other Little People who had faced discrimination or assumptions, for the dogs themselves. But there was still tons of work to be done, and I sure as hell couldn't do it behind bars 'cause I'd been stupid enough to drink and drive.

I had to be strong. I had to be a warrior. There was a wolf in the woods, and he was hungry. He was being blamed for terrorizing not just the city, but the entire world. In France and in the UK, they were banning "bully" breeds in their entirety. President Bush signed legislation forbidding military personnel and their families from having pit bulls as pets on any military base, national or international. Someone had to stand up, like St. Francis did for the wolf. Someone had to do something. It was me. I was the one who had to do something.

I had to convince Animal Planet to let me go global. We needed to march on Denver, then shoot in Mexico, protest the pit bull bans in France, draw attention to the bully breed ban in the American military by traveling to Afghanistan or Iraq with the USO. I'd heard from soldiers that in Afghanistan they were hawking pirated copies of *Pit Boss* with Arabic subtitles. We had guys that were putting their lives on the line for our country. Guys that had lost a leg or an eye, and they had to give away their dogs? There were stories to share from every far-flung corner of the universe. I had to get out there and tell them.

Animal Planet had a different idea.

9

Welcome
Home

started to receive a flood of mail from fans wanting to know more about my personal life. The show was focused primarily on the business and the dogs, but I had talked about Dad on the show a lot. People wanted to see this man. Letters came in saying, "We know you're an ex-con, we know you had a rough childhood, we know you can be a fucking ass, we know you love pit bulls, but we want you to go home." And by "go home" they meant they wanted *Pit Boss* to film a reunion episode with my family, specifically with my father.

Animal Planet and Intuitive knew about the letters and encouraged me to think about a visit, but I wasn't talking to my dad at all. My sister Janet still held hatred for him. I told her, "Come on, Janet, give it up and just let it go. We can't change nothing about our past, nothing about who he is, nothing about their marriage. We just have to accept who he is." That was my position. There was no outright hatred on my part, but there was no energy to make things better either, and I certainly had no interest in shooting a reunion episode! I was convinced that would be a fiasco!

Now, a good son is supposed to honor his parents, but it's hard to do that when you don't have a relationship. I hadn't seen my parents in well over two years. I had tried to connect with Mom a few times. I'd e-mailed her a bunch of questions, and I got back a response that largely ignored my e-mail and just said, "Glad you're doing good. Dad just did this and Dad just did that . . ." Clearly, he was still standing behind her telling her what to write. It got to the point that when I'd call, Dad would stand over her and monitor the call 'cause Mom had the tendency to blab, like mothers do. I'd hear him whisper in the background. "Don't tell him I fell in the kitchen. I'll feel like a dumbass." Shit, I ran into things all the time. I didn't care if he fell. Why couldn't we just talk like normal people? So e-mailing and calling didn't work. Visits didn't either. Dad would offer to buy me a ticket to come out on the condition that I had to spend a week with them. I didn't have a week to give up to being locked up in the middle of nowhere. I was running two businesses and shooting a TV show. Dad had no sense of my reality at all. I just gave up trying to connect.

I knew Dad had seen a few episodes of the show. He knew what I had said about him. Janet told me he was upset about it. Linda apparently couldn't wait to break the news that my life was part of the show. She told them that I was talking about my time in prison, about my childhood. Dad's comment was, "How can he do that to us?" To them! I was the little fucker that spent ten years in prison. It wasn't his story to tell, but he took it personally and he certainly never understood how I could see being in prison as a positive thing. There was just no way either one of us was going to agree to shoot a show. I didn't wanna put Mom and Dad on the air and pretend that everything was okay between us just because people were curious. It would have been a lie.

But the letters kept coming in. Intuitive and Animal Planet really wanted to acknowledge and honor the fan requests. We went back and forth for six months about it, and my resolve began to waver. Didn't I owe it to my fans to listen to their letters? Finally, I called Janet to see what she thought, and she kind of talked me into making the trip just to check up on Mom. I decided to go to Texas.

But I couldn't tell Animal Planet and Intuitive that! Sneaky me, I had a bargaining chip and I was going to use it. I said, "Okay, if I get on a plane to Texas then I wanna do a segment in Mexico. If people want to know more about me, they need to see why I've chosen to live part-time down there, to see what we do there." It only made sense to film in Mexico. Mexico was a home for me. It was my sanctuary. In Mexico, I wasn't the Pit Boss. I was just some crazy gringo with a bunch of dogs. If there's one thing I've learned from living in the projects and being in prison . . . just 'cause people have money and almost everything they want, it doesn't mean they are happy. It's the people that don't have shit that learn to make themselves happy. I see this repeated over and over again. Our country doesn't realize how good we got it. I can be in lower-income neighborhoods, or in the poverty-stricken areas of Mexico, and at every meal, people eat together as a family. When they sit down for either lunch or dinner, it's an occasion. Every fucking day. They celebrate life. Everybody's happy, everybody's enjoying the moment. They have a drink. They eat. They beat the shit out of each other, then shake hands and forget it.

I wanted to show Americans that Mexico was not the horrible, blood-soaked battle zone that the constant negativity of the national news would have you believe. As I traveled around for pit bull awareness events, I was shocked at people's reaction to me living there part-time. They'd stand up and ask, "Why would you put yourself and your dogs in danger by living in Mexico?" These were pit bull advocates and owners and lovers. I'd respond, "Where do you get that information, that it's dangerous?" They'd reply, "You hear about it all the time on TV." And this is when I'd get angry. "You mean, how like you hear all the time on TV that pit bulls are dangerous?"

It was hypocritical. These people who were so clear that the media was waging a war against pit bulls would turn right around and believe them about Mexico. No, Mexico is not the safest country in the world. But neither is America. I leave my doors unlocked in Mexico. I don't do that in L.A. You are more likely to get hit by a random shot in America than you are by a random gunshot in Mexico. Yes, there are serious things going on in Mexico in serious areas, just like there are in the United States. Would you go wandering around the Nickerson projects at three o'clock in the morning? No. You'd probably be robbed. So, in Mexico, you stay away from the border towns. You stay away from the cities and places that are having problems. It's a big country. If there's a shooting in Chicago, you don't cancel your trip to Miami.

■ ■ ■

Animal Planet held up their end of the bargain, and we shot in Mexico. I was really happy that I got to show a more personal side of my life, that my fans could see that my home in Mexico was safe, and that they got to meet my Mexican friends, like Juan, who was raised at the Doors of Faith Orphanage. Intuitive let us shoot at the orphanage, and spend time with the kids there. We brought them food and cooking supplies, and I even snuck in some candy. It was important to me that we got to show our fans that we're helping pit bulls in America and pit bulls in Mexico, but we also help kids . . . on both sides of the border. Most people think I'm so single-minded about rescuing pit bulls, but I can be a real sucker for kids. If someone hands me a baby, I'll even put my wine down and my cigar out—and that's saying something.

When we got back to the States, it was my turn. Texas was on the production schedule. When Intuitive first contacted Dad, he was all gung-ho about it. I was shocked that he'd agreed to us shooting down there without a big argument. Then he watched a few more episodes of the show, where I was bashing the shit out of him, and he changed his mind.

It's not that he accused me of lying or slander. My dad doesn't deny that he maintained an abusive household, and even if he did deny it, I have proof. I have my sisters. They lived it, too. It's just that Dad can't stand airing the family's dirty laundry. Me, I don't hide nothing. His argument against me blabbing was, "I put a roof over your head. I gave you clothes on your back, food on the table." My point was, "None of that matters if you don't feel loved. None of that matters if you're miserable and being hit."

The production company had booked all of the tickets and hotels. We were supposed to leave in four days. Dad called and said, "No. You're not coming down here." The whole trip was canceled. Plane tickets, hotels, car rentals, everything. The producers, Jodi and Carlos, weren't giving up that easy. I told them, "You're gonna have to promise him that you won't film certain things. You're gonna have to play by his rules." One of his rules was that we could not film in the house. So we were gonna fly all the way to Texas to shoot a reunion show where we would not be able to film in the actual house? The producers said yes to everything, just to get him to agree. Jodi and Carlos did everything in their power to accommodate his demands, but Dad would agree to things then have too much time to think them over. He was indecisive. He canceled again.

On the third attempt, Jodi and Carlos wised up. They had me call and try to reason with him. I called Mom and said, "I'm gonna be in Austin leading a protest and a march. We can come down and put you on the show and visit. Why don't we just play it day by day?" I made it sound very casual, but Intuitive was tired of taking Dad at his word. Who could blame them? They required this time that Dad sign a waiver committing him to the shoot. Why fly all the way out there just to have him cancel everything at the last minute?

Once we got to Texas, I tried to warn Carlos and Jodi about how my parents were gonna be. They thought I should arrive at the house first, but I knew better. I knew the production team needed to go first. Dad would have a bunch of rules to lay down about what they could and couldn't do. "You can't shoot in the house." "You can't mike us." Dad was so paranoid about being recorded that he would yell at guys on the production team if they tried to use their cell phones. He thought they were taping him somehow. He needed to be in complete control.

So I sat in a taxi, around the corner, for an hour and a half, waiting to get the all clear to show up at the house. I was miked, even though they weren't. I got the call to drive up, and when I saw that sign hanging over the house, "Welcome Home Shorty," I couldn't believe it. They'd been waiting for me to come home. How long had they had that sign? Was it fake? Was it sincere? Was it for the show?

I stepped out of the taxi and was surprised to see my dad was using a walker. He'd had recent back surgery, but considering it took him until he was seventy to have back problems, he was doing pretty well. It struck me how much he'd aged. I almost kind of let my guard down to see him like that, but then I realized he was still the same guy. He still wouldn't take no for an answer. He wouldn't ask for help.

Sometimes these things I say about Dad, that he never took no for an answer, that he did everything his own way, that he always had to be in control, that he had a temper, that he was overly aggressive, determined . . . it's like looking in the fucking mirror. I'm talking about my own damn self. We talked a bit outside before Dad insisted that we go inside. No cameras! I was still miked, so the cameras could hear every word I was saying. Dad and Mom took me on a tour of the house. This wasn't the house I grew up in. This was more of a ranch, with several acres of land attached. They had moved since I was a kid. I was just trying to get along. I didn't wanna ruin a good thing. We seemed to be back on good terms. He had a few things that he'd made for me. A desk caddy that holds pens and pencils. A temperature gauge that was made out of spare car parts. It turned out to be a good visit and it was good to see Mom.

I thought maybe we'd come to some sort of truce, but that was just my wishful thinking. After the episode aired, my sister Linda started stirring up trouble again. Linda was living in Kansas City and working as a dog groomer. She'd always been a dog lover. She'd always had animals. From the get-go. Mom and Linda spoke on a pretty regular basis, so I knew she watched the show. Mom told me. I was waiting for her to contact me. We hadn't spoken since 2000. I was surprised it took so long.

Linda saw the episode and she was pissed. Linda was mortified that I'd said on-air that she wasn't Dad's kid, that Dad wanted nothing to do with her, and that he considered her a stepchild. I didn't see what was wrong with saying that. It was the truth. She was still my mom's kid. She was still my half sister. It didn't change the fact that we're family, even if we don't get along.

She sent a letter to Intuitive saying, "You people have no right to blur my photo." When we shot in Texas, we shot a family photo, but we didn't have a signed release from Linda to use the image, so we had to blur her face. We didn't do it to exclude her from the family story. It wasn't meant to be hurtful. That's just standard legal procedure on any film or documentary or TV show or whatever. The only people who don't have to do that are news operations, and even they do it sometimes. Her letter went on and on, telling me that I "would be refused to attend her funeral." After we got that letter, Intuitive suggested I reunite with Linda.

Dear God.

Here we go again.

No, thanks!

The reunion was a big hit with my fans and was good for ratings, but it didn't change our family dynamic. I called a couple of times afterward, and things went right back to the way they'd been. Dad would hover over Mom on the phone. He was still recovering from his back surgery, walking with a fucking walker or canes or crutches, and his dumb ass got up on a ladder to paint the eaves of the house. So he fell, broke his shoulder and his jaw. They had to wire his jaw shut, which must have been a relief for Mom. But she got "in trouble" for e-mailing me about it. He was so embarrassed. "You're not supposed to tell anyone nothing without checking with me first!" How he yelled through that wire jaw, I don't know. I dread the day when I get a phone call telling me they've blown each other to bits with a shotgun.

My fans probably believe we're closer and in touch now, but the only communication we have is through Facebook. My mom keeps tabs on me and I see her respond to my posts. Dad doesn't understand Facebook—he's Facebook-challenged—and that allows Mom to interact with me without being censored by him. There are days when I wish things could be different between us, and in the future, anything is possible. People are capable of change. I'm living proof of that, but as for my dad, I'm not holding my breath.

■ ■ ■

With Mexico and Texas under our belts, and with *Pit Boss* renewed for another season and our ratings rising, I felt like I finally had enough juice to tackle Denver. The power of the media had to be harnessed in a positive way, to let people know about breed-specific legislation and how useless it really is. BSL accomplishes nothing. It doesn't improve public safety, or even prevent dog bites. It's expensive. It does nothing to hold irresponsible dog owners accountable for their actions, while at the same time punishing responsible dog owners, and here's the kicker: Not one single animal welfare organization supports the policy. Not one.

Now that *Pit Boss* had been picked up for international distribution, I knew our filming in Denver could have real impact. Before, I wasn't sure we could make a difference. We could have marched through the streets naked, screaming our fool heads off, but we would have just been preaching to the choir. The people in Denver already know about the issue. We would have been covered by the local news at best. It was the larger national and international response I wanted to incite. I wanted to shine a brighter light.

I hired a lawyer before the protest. We'd been in touch, and she was one of the reasons I wanted to do the Denver trip. She was helping me in Miami as well. She filed lawsuits on my behalf against both cities for the right to travel with Hercules, my service animal. Years before, when Allison was still working for Shortywood, she'd had to oversee a gig in Miami 'cause of the ban. I couldn't travel to the gig, and that had always bothered me. I'd always wanted to right that wrong. Here was my chance to say, "I have a service animal. You've banned my dog. You're keeping me from traveling. That's my constitutional right. I'm coming after you."

The lawyer helped connect me with several rescue organizations in the Denver area, and we organized a march on City Hall, an awareness/fund-raising event at a local bar, an event in nearby Colorado Springs with PETA, and an appearance before the city council members. My hopes were tempered. This is legislation that has been in effect for over twenty years, so I knew we weren't going to change things overnight. A march, a fund-raiser, a lawsuit . . . these were the first steps in a marathon. A marathon I'll win. Even if Hercules has to carry me over the finish line.

As soon as we announced our plans, a bunch of e-mails were sent to my website: "Don't come to Denver. We will shoot you." Or, "I'm coming to the protest. You better watch out. You better take care of yourself. There better be someone standing in front of you." The only person on my team that knew about the e-mails was Julie, 'cause she was the one who opened them up. Neither Seb nor Ron nor Ashley knew nothing about this. Julie brought a few of the e-mails to my attention. "You need to be aware of these." So then I asked her to put me in the loop and show me what she saw. She asked, "Do you really wanna do this?"

We'd started to have our fair share of fanatical fans and had had to call security on people before, so I didn't take these threats lightly. I had a guy one time try to steal my hat. Just ran up and pulled it off my head. The more popular the show became, the more dangerous it had become to be the face of pit bull advocacy. There are still people who truly believe that pit bulls are killing machines. They have enzymes to kill, they are bred to kill . . . these are their beliefs. They see me as a baby killer.

This is why I always travel with mace and a Taser, no matter where I go. If it's a public event, there are always hundreds of people and dogs. People aren't always in control of their dogs (or themselves), and on a hot day, in a crowd with people drinking, you never know what they may or may not do. People can get stupid, and I need to be able to defend myself and my dogs. If I have to break up a dogfight, or a dog attacks Hercules, or an adamant fan comes after me, I am always suited to booted, carrying some sort of protection, and Juan, my personal assistant, is always suited to booted as well. We've never had to use the mace or the Tasers, and I hope we never have to, but eventually, if everything keeps going the way it is, I know I will need to get a bodyguard. The more we provoke and stir up controversy, the more dangerous the job becomes. Plus, my lovely personality and anger issues don't help at all.

I never told Animal Planet or Intuitive about any of the security issues we faced at events. It was better not to freak them out, so I certainly didn't tell them about the Denver death threats, for fear they would cancel the march, the fundraiser, or even the whole trip. I didn't even tell the team in my office. Nobody knew. In fact, the producers still don't know about those death threats. Unless they're reading this book.

If shit was gonna happen, then it would happen. I didn't want people to be concerned. Getting this information to the world was more important than anything. People had no idea how horrible the situation was, and still is, in Denver. We had those photos of dead dogs in barrels, and we couldn't put them on TV—they were too graphic. I wasn't going to back down over a couple of nasty e-mails.

I decided I needed to wear a bulletproof vest. I bought one for me, and even got one for Hercules. His shit cost sixteen-hundred dollars! Christ. While we were traveling, I had my bulletproof vest, my Taser, and my mace in one particular suitcase, and I wouldn't let anyone else handle that bag except me. My producer was getting curious about the suitcase. I couldn't tell him it was a bulletproof vest 'cause then he'd know what was going on.

Since I was traveling with Hercules, I couldn't fly directly into Denver. I had to fly into Colorado Springs, rent a car, drive for two hours, and stay outside the city limits so I could be with him. One of the producers wanted me to take Hercules into Denver, but there was no way I was gonna put my dog in danger. If they had killed my dog, I would have had to kill the producer.

Each one of my six pit bulls is family to me. They each have their own personality, their own voice. They are completely different from one another. Hercules can't stand being left alone. Geisha would rather be outside in the backyard with the sun. Mussolini would rather be on the roof barking at the world. Domenico can't stay out of trouble—he's so busy trying to escape. Valentino just loves to roughhouse and play with the rest of the dogs. Bebi is my Mexican jumping bean— she wants all the attention.

They are a very smart pack. I came home one time and found all six dogs, drunk and sprawled out all over the floor. Between them they had figured out how to open the refrigerator door, crack open the beers, and have a party. I found empty beer cans in every corner of the room . . . twelve total. I put a lock on the refrigerator. I thought that would do it.

Nope.

In Mexico, the house has hard tile floors and no carpets, which is much better for a house full of dogs; much cleaner. I had stacked a few cases of wine near the kitchen, and one day, I came home to find a broken wine bottle on the floor. I thought it fell, or the dogs knocked it over. I did, however, think it was suspicious that there was no actual wine on the floor. Then it happened again. Then it happened a third time, and this time, I caught them in the act. Mussolini grabbed a bottle of wine in his mouth and slammed it to the ground while all the other dogs waited around for the goods. I hopped out. "Aha!" Mussolini had red wine dripping down his chest. Bebi had red all over her mouth and Geisha wouldn't look me in the eye.

I wasn't mad. I love them. It's like something kids do. Sneak a sip of your drink. Do something devious. Just to see if they can get away with it. I find it hilarious. (But not when they tear through drywall or Valentino destroys the leather couch.) One day he chewed through plaster, ripped the couch open, destroyed the remote control, and got in the garbage can. That was not so hilarious.

But I have to admit that out of all my dogs, I have two favorites. Geisha is my girl. She's been with me from the beginning, and she's been the most important to me. She's the one that got me interested in advocacy and breed awareness. She's the one who inspired me to fight to save the dogs. She's the reason I'm doing what I do now. But then, I also wanna give it to Hercules, 'cause he's become the poster child of every pit bull in this world. He's showing the world who these dogs really are and who they can be when they are well trained and loved. Everywhere we go, Hercules gets more attention than me. He's become a symbol of this struggle. He's got those big eyes and a gentle, playful demeanor. He can just sit there and pretend like he's better than every human being. Whether he knows it or not, he's actually done more for this breed than a lot of humans in this world have done.

So, no, I wasn't going to endanger Hercules's life to prove a point in Denver, but it sucked being without him. My back was really acting up. I had to use a cane, and I felt like an idiot. When you don't use a cane on a regular basis, you don't know how to maneuver. I fell on my ass a couple of times.

I just put the vest on under my clothes, and it was cold enough out that I wore my trench coat so no one could tell I had it on. I was trying to concentrate on the march and the reason I was there, but at the same time, in the back of my mind, I was thinking, "Are these guys serious?" We got through the march peacefully, then I was allowed to speak to the council members.

These are the same council people who voted to ban pit bulls twenty years ago. They are still there, sitting like rigid skeletons in their chairs. They have never been around pit bulls and they've never personally witnessed pit bull aggression or attacks. They have their opinions based on nothing, and they refuse to listen to anybody else's point of view. They're power hungry, and they like their feelings of self-righteousness. I told them: "You have a one-in-twenty-five-million chance of being bitten by a dog, and of those bites that do happen, only six to eight percent are pit bulls. You have a one-in-twelve chance of being a victim of crime. So, who are you chasing? The wrong animal!"

I kept going. "I have twenty-plus years of experience dealing with this breed. I've witnessed every bad thing that can happen and every good thing that can happen. The only thing I've never seen is a human being attacked by a pit bull. I have never seen a pit turn on a human, and I have never been bitten by a pit myself."

I was on my soapbox and loving it. "And just like kids who've had a shitty life and end up in trouble can be re-formed, and go on to be loving, productive people in society, so can dogs who've been trained to fight. They can be reha-bilitated. The majority of Michael Vick's dogs that were used for fighting or used for bait were placed in homes with other dogs or with other kids. I've met quite a few of the people who own them. It's not the dogs that should be put down. It's the humans."

I have no idea if they actually heard a single word I said. Some people hear only what they want to hear, words that support their own opinions. Everything else just sounds like . . . *blah, blah, blah.*

It is one thing to march and make speeches. It's another thing to make it personal. We had an owner named Louise who had to give up her pit. We had to sneak the dog out of the city and she was bawling her eyes out. The dog was howling and crying. I knew the emotionality of it all would be good for the episode, but it was too much for me to take. It was painful to watch.

It's one thing for people to hear about the bans. It's another thing for them to see the bans in action. If they can visualize it, they are more likely to act. With Louise crying and the dog howling, it touched people's hearts. That was the moment that caused people to pick up their phones and write letters. The response to the Denver episode was swift. We were swamped with e-mails. People were pissed. I posted the address of the councilmen so people could e-mail them directly, and send letters supporting our protest. I'll print it here again now. Let the city of Denver know how you feel. Let them hear it from the rest of the country. From the world.

> Councilman Charlie Brown, Cached City Council,
>   District 6
> City and County Building
> 1437 Bannock St., Rm. 451
> Denver, CO 80202
> Phone: 720-865-9534
> Fax: 720-865-9540
> E-mail: dencc@denvergov.org
> www.denvergov.org/charliebrown

Tell Charlie Brown that the demonization of pit bulls is unfair; that punishing responsible owners for the actions of a few is no basis for creating a law. Tell him that it's a proven fact that BSL does not reduce the number of dog bites or the incidence of fatal attacks. Tell him that in the UK, dog bites actually increased fifty percent after the Dangerous Dog Act passed in 1997. Tell him that in Prince George's County, Maryland, a task force studied the effects of the county's BSL policy, and found that the law cost taxpayers $250,000 a year, with no positive effect on public safety. Tell him that the Centers for Disease Control, the American Veterinary Medical Association, and the National Animal Control Association all oppose breed-specific legislation.

Then tell him he can kiss Shorty's little white ass.

10
The
Boss

Lieutenant Dave from Long Beach Animal Control called to tell me that he'd just rescued a pit bull from the back of an empty house. A neighbor reported the dog as abandoned. After twelve years of being the beloved family pet, the family had moved and left their dog behind. When he showed me the picture, she looked like Hercules and Geisha. She had the same coloring and eyes. She was old and covered in bedsores. I couldn't stand it. I said, "You know what? I'm taking her. I don't know what the fuck I'm gonna do with her, but I'm taking her." There was just no way I could let that pretty girl, who might die tomorrow of old age, die alone. She belonged with a family. I put a call in to one of my rescue groups, and we found a retirement home for old dogs. I picked her up and took her to her new home, where she could live out the rest of her days in peace, and surrounded by new friends.

It's moments like that that confuse the hell out of me. I don't understand humans. How could a family do that? The dog was there for them for twelve years, and they just left her there to die. If they weren't allowed to bring the dog to their new home, they could hide the dog in the car, sneak the dog in, find somebody else to keep her, do something. Even dropping the dog off at a rescue organization or a no-kill facility is not a solution. Money doesn't grow on trees, and these shelters are at maximum capacity all the time. People try to drop off their dogs, but aren't willing to make a donation to the shelter, and then get mad when they're told that there's no more room at the inn.

I could open up a kennel for two thousand pit bulls, and within two weeks, I'd be full, with no potential homes for the dogs, and the overhead of having to feed, water, clean, and care for them. If I kept my doors open, I'd have ten thousand dogs in a few months. I'd have to win an eighty-million-dollar jackpot to open up and run a facility. It's the only way we could be self-sufficient, and not have to rely on the random donations of caring people.

It's frustrating to wake each day and find yet one more example of human cruelty, but rescuing dogs will always be a part of who I am, just like performing and entertainment will always be my career. The business of "the business" may drive me crazy, but I make my living as an entertainer, and being a talent manager has financially supported my cause of pit bull advocacy. The two are intertwined and inseparable in me. I can't turn either of those aspects of my personality off, and why would I want to? Dogs and Hollywood have been good to me. They gave me a purpose. They gave me a second chance. They saved my life.

It's not an act. People think I carry a bat, climb fences, smash windows, or break into cars to save the dogs on *Pit Boss* 'cause it's dramatic. Or they think I'm being told by the producers to act that way. To me, it doesn't matter if the cameras are rolling or not, if there's a pit bull in trouble, I'm gonna smash shit, I'm gonna climb shit, I'm gonna break shit to get to her. That bat is always in my car, or by my front door. I could probably sell it on eBay for a small fortune, but I don't need a producer to tell me to use it. The only thing the cameras do is keep me from being arrested. They come in handy when somebody calls the cops.

Do I have to pick my battles when I approach with my bat? Yeah, now that I'm a public figure, I do. Nike has just signed an endorsement deal with Michael Vick. People want me to protest this. A year or so ago, Burger King came out with a commercial stereotyping pit bulls and Rottweilers. I went on the TV news in San Diego to protest it. I had Hercules pee on the Burger King sign. Our local segment was picked up by the national news. The next day, I was in fucking trouble. Even though I have the right to take a stance, I can't protest a company that's paying my network. They don't have ads on Animal Planet, but they were supporting twelve other channels owned by Discovery. It got from the top of Burger King to the top of Discovery like . . . *bang*. We went into crisis-management mode. They had a huge meeting about it. I got a lecture.

It comes down to a choice of staying on the air or fighting with Burger King. I have to choose my battles. It's the same thing that's happening with Nike right now. If we are cancelled, then we don't have a way to reach a larger audience. I'm between a rock and a hard place. Do you think you can destroy a multinational company with one piss on a sign? I know I can't. I have to think of the bigger picture. How can I serve the dogs? Nike is a national sponsor. I'm under the gun. I understand now what it is like to have to hide out from fans or to bow to corporate sponsors. Just 'cause I am not commenting on Nike. No matter what I say, half of the people will hate me, and half of the people will love me. That's who I've always been, and that's who I'll always be.

And yeah, I scream at my employees, and demand perfection out of them. Anyone who works for me, I tell them, "You can wear jeans, but you better have on nice shoes and a dress shirt. You are a representative of me." These are my rules. They're basically the same rules I typed up as a kid, when I was daydreaming about my British butler and my executive suite. I expect nothing less out of them than what I expect out of myself. I hold them to the same standards. I want them to work hard or go home. If I was soft-spoken and didn't yell and had unlimited patience and didn't push the people around me, I would not have a company. I would've gone bankrupt, and I sure as hell wouldn't be on TV.

I'm the boss. I'm living proof that when you have a dream, you can do it. No matter what it is. Do it! It was my dream to be a businessman in the corporate world. Well, maybe I'm not in the corporate world, but here I am. I accomplished the business side of the damn thing. I've used Facebook and social networks to build my business. Not too many people get their own reality show, and turn around and market it to make real change; to have a lasting impact on the world. I wasn't built to be a manager at Best Buy or Walmart. I wasn't built to be political. I understand that I've been built to be the face of this movement. That everything I've lived through in my life has prepared me and propelled me into this job, the job of promoting the breed.

Looking back, I understand that who I am today was created by what I went through. If I hadn't had a father who was a fucking ass, if I hadn't run away to live in the projects, if I didn't go to prison, I wouldn't be who I am today. I was a work in progress. My greatest triumph in life has been being me. First of all, I'm not dead. From the day that I was born, I've proven everyone wrong. So why not just keep proving them wrong over and over and over again?

No matter how bad your life is, it can get better. There were guys in prison who couldn't handle being there. They killed themselves. Hung themselves from the tiers. They couldn't see that there was an ending, that things could be better. I never considered jail to be my defeat. My life wasn't over. I was young and I knew I'd be out at a young age. On those days, in the hole, when it seemed like hours stretched into eternity, I'd think about Nelson Mandela. He didn't know he was going home. He didn't know he was gonna rule the country. Just 'cause someone is a gangbanger doesn't mean he can't come out on top. I always knew there was something better waiting for me outside those prison bars. I didn't know it was pit bulls. I didn't know it was Hollywood. But I'm grateful for both.

There will come a day when *Pit Boss* won't be on the air, but I'm not going away. I'll still be doing what I do. The show just gives me a platform to reach more people, and let them know what's going on with pit bulls and Little People. But once the show is over, I will still be out in the world, doing what I do. *Pit Boss* has lit a fire underneath me. It's brought me face-to-face with the enormity of the true and profound effect that pit bulls have on people. They are the most hated breed of dog in the world. I knew it was bad. I just never realized it was this bad.

That's why my goal is to keep promoting the breed on a much bigger scale. I used the lessons that Dan Kolsrud taught me on the set of *Daddy Day Care* to produce *Hercules Saves Christmas*, a family movie for Christmastime, starring Hercules as Santa's "Naughty and Nice List Maker." Hercules was following in the paw prints of Petey from the *Little Rascals*, and I wanted to reestablish that pit bulls could star in family-friendly fare, without being the murderous, barking, foaming-at-the-mouth, dangerous dog next door. I didn't expect one made-for-TV movie to change minds overnight, but I knew it was a good start. As soon as we wrapped principal photography, I started plotting out the sequel.

I also went back down to Nicaragua and asked A.J. if we could come out with a full line of cigars. We already had the Diesel Shorty, but I wanted to add two more cigars, the Shorty

Punisher and the San Bajito (Saint Shorty) to the mix. I also teamed with Wilson Creek Winery to create the Shorty Rossi Merlot. All the proceeds from the sales would literally go to the dogs, to ensure that our rescue operation could keep running, whether or not we had a weekly show on the air.

That's the most important thing. To give something back, no matter what it is. You have to do something else to help out human or animal kind. Whether you are adopting kids, volunteering at the Red Cross, or the Salvation Army, or your church, you have to give back something to this world. To actually be considered a success, you gotta give a shit.

It was prison that got me thinking that way. First, with the anger management classes and victim awareness classes, but also having gone through the DUI courses really drilled that thinking into my brain. I could see that my life affected other people's lives. My choices affected other's people's happiness.

That bystander I accidently shot all those years ago, I wonder if he knows who I am today. I'm not five-foot-eight with brown hair, so I would assume he would recognize me at some point, though I doubt very seriously he's paid attention to where I landed. Would I ever look him up? No. Why not? Maybe he wants to shoot me back, I don't know. I wouldn't blame him if he did. He may still hold rage against me. Some people are capable of hate for their entire lives. But I hope he would see that I've truly changed as a person, and that I hope I can improve the world, not just for Little People or for pit bulls, but maybe inspire people to believe in their own redemption.

We are all capable of great things, but sometimes we forget

that about ourselves. We get wrapped up in our lives when outside the doors of the house, so much shit is going on. It doesn't have to be pit bulls. It can be a bird sanctuary. It can be volunteering at the fucking zoo. It can be taking care of an elderly neighbor, or helping some kid who's in trouble. It shouldn't take an 8.0 earthquake or a tsunami to help the next man out. We should be doing it all the time.

We should be helping each other rise.

Epilogue

So, you can't say I didn't warn you.

Page One, I warned you.

I've got a mouth and I use it.

It makes me friends.

It creates enemies.

Whether you are friend or foe, that's up to you.

This is just the truth of who I am.

The man I've been, the man I've become, and the man I still
hope to be.

Who do I hope to be?

I hope to be like Valentino. Able to chew through obstacles,
rip through the walls that hold me back, nose my way into
every dark corner to root out the wrong and make it right.

I hope to be like Domenico. Running wild and free through the world, showing those old corrections officers what a real escape artist looks like, unbound by the chains of my past.

I hope to be like Mussolini. Howling until I'm hoarse, and howling some more, so I make sure everyone knows exactly what I think . . . and, you know, smashing a few wine bottles now and then, to cover my mug in merlot.

I hope to be like Bebi. More openhearted, loving, and cuddlier than I look.

I hope to be like Geisha. Mellowing with age, to become a grumpy old crank that grays around the temples and farts in inappropriate places, without apology.

But mostly, I hope to be like Hercules. Steady, present, and able to bear the burden of this battle on broad shoulders, with patience and grace.

That's who I hope to be.

A man as noble as a pit bull.

If I can do that, turn out anything like my dogs . . . I'll be proud.

Essential Shorty

On Love and Relationships

Once you go small, you will never go tall!

What freaky stuff goes on in Shorty's bedroom stays in Shorty's bedroom.

I prefer to date taller women. I love the climbing technique. It makes getting the prize more interesting.

On Work

Get the hell out of my office!

I sweet talk, I con, I hustle, but I never give up.

On Being a Little Person

Little people get their revenge on tall people when Hercules farts in the elevator!

I have only dated two Little People women in my life. I call one the Bride of Chucky and the other one Psycho Bitch.

I came to the conclusion that it is okay to slap a Little Person when he tells your wife her hair smells pretty.

Four foot nine is too tall to be short and too short to be tall. Those guys are just screwed.

I may look harmless . . . until I grab your cojones.

I love going to a crowded mall, it gives me the chance to look at a good piece of ass and not get caught.

On Other People

I just can't understand how many stupid people we've got in this world.

I wish you would!

Everyone deserves a second chance . . . as long as they're trying to change.

Are you serious?

On Where He's Been . . .

I came from my mama's womb and my daddy's nuts!

If Hercules could write a book, I'd be in big trouble.

and Where He's Going

Watch out, world, here I come!

Life will take you places you've never expected to go.

Don't take life for granted when things are going good.

On Activism

One pit bull at a time.

Why aren't we punishing the humans instead of the pit bulls?

The people who run the city of Denver might as well be called Nazis!

Dogs don't talk shit back.

If the dog's on a plane, it's not a dog that's gonna bite you. Pet the fucking dog.

You can rescue all the pit bulls you want, but if you are not promoting the breed, you are doing nothing to change people's minds about adopting the breed!

On Religion

A Quinceañera? Isn't that when the young girls lose their virginity?

One time, I was at confession and the priest asked if I had my flask on me.

Acknowledgments

I would like to thank...

Everyone at Random House for letting the world know more about me and who I am. You've made my dream come true. Special thanks to Julia Pastore on the Random House team.

SJ Hodges, the person who caught the words that came out of my mouth and put them on the page.

Maura Teitelbaum, the agent who gave me a chance.

Everyone at Animal Planet, especially Majoric Kaplan, Rick Holzman, Erin Wannor, Tahli Kouperstein, Michael Eisenbaum, and Amaryllis Seabrooks. You've given me the chance to speak to the world, and you continue to help me every day.

My producers at Intuitive. You never give up on me. Special thanks to Mechelle Collins and Kevin Dill. And for the entire production team, who has no choice but to put up with me, especially Jodi Baskerville.

My family, especially my sister Janet Burton and uncle Charles Bailey.

Acknowledgments

My friends who have been with me before I was Pit Boss, and now, including Juan Antonio Vidal Castillo, Ron and Nadine de Yong, Dawn Tarr, Linda Distante, Sam Clemente, Clay Roberts, Alex Svenson, Debbie Carrabello, Jerry Lucas (RIP), Hank Pervis Henderson, Derek Zemrak, Dan Brunning, Allison Queal, Jack Selby, Eduardo and Diana Aviles, Steve Dunn, Little Darlin, and Jeff.

My Shortywood Team. My employees and friends, you need a special mention: Ashley Brooks, Candy Clemente, Julie Marie Hernandez, Liz Fiano, Marcos Ramirez Hernandez, Brayan Castillo Borjas, Alma Castillo, Alexander Nah.

The corrections officers, counselors, and prison employees that gave me a second chance, including Celia Cruz-Reed, Vic Federico, Judy Nahigian, Jones Moore, Don Reynolds, Sonia Miller, Steve Larson, Lieutenant Centurino, Gary Gonzales (Gee), Larry Mackey, Mike Gallegos.

My legal team. You make life a little easier on me. Jeff Cohen, Craig Stien, Pilar Villazón, Tammy Vo Hamilton.

The guys I did time with. You always had my back: Tony Carrabello, Roger Clark, Kevin Fuqua, Ray Benard, Irby Davis, Lefty, J-Rock, Noel "Do-Low" Pinnock, Michael "Snake" Aaron, Odell (Big O), Big Will, Big Will (ii), Lawrence (L-Dogg), Green Eyes, Big Ike, Little Will, Sexton Davis.

And finally, thank you to my priest, Father William Raymond. It always takes his entire afternoon to hear my confession.

About the Author

Shorty Rossi is the star of Animal Planet's *Pit Boss*; the owner of Shortywood Entertainment, a talent management company for Little People; and the owner of Shorty's Pit Bull Rescue.

www.shortywood.com